Thank you and
God bless you!
Franklin & Doris Burns
12-8-16

BEYOND POSSUM KINGDOM

ADVENTURES OF FAITH WITH AN AWESOME GOD

FRANKLIN & DORIS BURNS

WESTBOW®
PRESS
A DIVISION OF THOMAS NELSON
& ZONDERVAN

Scripture taken from the New King James Version. Copyright © 1979, 1980, 1982 by Thomas Nelson, Inc. Used by permission. All rights reserved.

WestBow Press books may be ordered through booksellers or by contacting:

WestBow Press
A Division of Thomas Nelson & Zondervan
1663 Liberty Drive
Bloomington, IN 47403
www.westbowpress.com
1 (866) 928-1240

ISBN: 978-1-4908-5317-8 (sc)
ISBN: 978-1-4908-5318-5 (hc)
ISBN: 978-1-4908-5319-2 (e)

Library of Congress Control Number: 2014916932

Printed in the United States of America.

WestBow Press rev. date: 10/14/2014

CONTENTS

PART 3 - WITH VISION COMES PROVISION

PART 4 - THE BLESSING OF DIVINE PROTECTION

PART 5 - THE AWESOME POWER OF OUR GOD

FOREWORD

To my parents:

From as far back as I can remember my parents have been a rock in my life. My Dad and Mom have been firm believers in faith and miracles. There is never anything too hard or unachievable in their eyes when God is in it. Through every step of ministry as I was growing up, we went from one miracle to another. I have always said that for me, miracles are not the end result; miracles are the process of what one goes through to get to the end result – which is just the celebration of the miracle.

At times there were things that were impossible, or seemed impossible, but for them, there was always an answer.

They have always supported us in our decisions in life regarding what we wanted to do. As we have traveled the world together, every experience has been nothing short of miraculous. I know when you read this book you will laugh, cry, rejoice and shout, and if you are expecting something from God, this book is definitely for you!

Mom and Dad, I love you with all of my heart and I thank you for raising me the way you did, because that is why I am who I am today. We have been asking you forever to write this book, so there are no words to describe how excited and happy we are!

Your daughter,
Wynelle

To my in-laws:

Franklin A Burns: A True Latin American Ambassador of Apostolic Faith.

I remember the first time I met Franklin and Doris Burns very well. I was invited to a revival service in Arlington, Texas. and asked by my host, "Do you know Franklin Burns?" I said, "Who?"

It didn't take long to find out who he was. What an impact he and his wife, Doris, made on me that night. Since then I have had the privilege of ministering with Franklin and Doris and have seen them mightily used by God.

Their exploits in God have given them an international ministry that has touched thousands. They are what God has made them – people of faith. Wherever you travel in Latin America you will see the tremendous ministry this couple has raised up. As you read this incredible book, I know you will be blessed and encouraged to step out in faith.

Your favorite son-in-law,
Dr. Paul

CHAPTER 1

Meet Franklin

For the last forty-five years I have endeavored to serve the Lord as a pioneer evangelist – going wherever He has led and, invariably, beginning with nothing – preaching the gospel and planting churches under His direction. Life has been unpredictable, exciting, and full of adventure, replete with the highs and lows of faith-stretching endeavor, but always full of blessing. In the face of unpredictability, our God has been and is continually steadfast and faithful.

Looking back, I am grateful for the Christian heritage I was blessed to receive, and which in no small part set me on the path that I have walked. My grandparents were ministers and also church planters, who pioneered a number of churches in their day. My parents were also pioneering, church planting evangelists. My father started many churches across the US – some twelve of them – before he passed away. Dad pioneered these dozen churches from scratch in the east and the south of the United States and he was on his way to starting a thirteenth, which he never got to finish. I am thankful that God saw fit to call me to carry on this wonderful legacy.

I grew up in a large family under challenging circumstances. There would eventually be nine of us kids in total – five girls and four boys. I was born in Florida, but our family left there soon after I was born, and made the journey across eight states in an old Model T Ford, to reach Fort Worth, Texas, where Dad and Mom were planting a new church.

This was during World War II and in 1942 we moved to some "accommodation" under the 7th Street Bridge, beside the Trinity River. Dad, Mom and their then eight kids, all living under a bridge! Life back then was almost unbelievable compared to today. As a child I remember my father tying ropes spanning column to column and then hanging blankets from them to create "walls", because there were other families sheltering under that bridge. It was some time before Dad found us an actual home in White Settlement, Fort Worth, and we began the new church.

Mom was eight months pregnant and it was very shortly before the ninth child was born that my father died. He became very ill, very suddenly and died of blood poisoning. Until then, no one had discovered that he was diabetic. It was six weeks before my sixth birthday. I was one of the youngest by some way, with brothers and sisters some twelve and fourteen years older than me.

But Mom was a hero of the faith. Faced with the enormous challenge of giving birth to a ninth child just a few weeks after losing her husband, and looking after eight other kids, she never failed. She took care of us and continued to raise each one of us faithfully. In due course, as a great testament to her faith and patient endurance, the majority of us would imitate our parents' dedication to the Lord and enter into ministry to serve as either pastors or missionaries.

Mom was a real prayer warrior. I don't recall any of us kids having the usual trips to the hospital with the sickness, broken bones or physical problems that many children have growing up. As soon as there was any sign of sickness, Mom would go to the Lord in prayer, anoint us and believe God for our healing. All I can say is, it worked! We all went on to have our own healthy families without complications.

My early life was lived in abject poverty. I remember many times when my sisters would cry themselves to sleep because they were so hungry and we had no food to eat. But, in the heart of our modest home in Fort Worth was the ever present, comforting warmth of a large potbellied stove, filled with firewood, which our family would gather around regularly to listen to the Word of God being read and to pray together.

Mom found a local church not too far away and we began to attend it faithfully. Pastor Ray Heady began a revival with a lady evangelist, coincidentally called Olive Burns. At the age of seven I recall going up to the altar and giving my heart to Jesus. The evangelist laid her hands on me and I was filled with the Holy Spirit. Several of my brothers and sisters were also saved and filled with the Holy Spirit at a young age.

I had just had my fourteenth birthday when God spoke to me very clearly and I knew His call on my life to preach the gospel according to Ephesians chapter 4. Pastor Ray was a godly man who had both the discernment to recognize God's call on me, and the foresight to give me the opportunity to begin preaching, even at that tender age. I was asked to preach at the Sunday night evangelistic service. To this day I still remember that first sermon and the scriptures I used. It will remain indelibly printed on my mind.

Our family lived on the north side of Fort Worth in an area called Goat Hill and this is where I began my ministry as a teenage boy. I heard about some tent revival meetings not too far from where we lived and felt prompted by God to go and attend, so I jumped on my bike and went to listen to the evangelist, Jack Coe. It was at one of these meetings that I had a significant experience with God and He graciously allowed me a glimpse of the vision He had for my future.

I stood at the back of the tent listening, looking at the sawdust all over the floor. Then I heard God speak to me, saying, "Look around you at this tent. One day you will travel the world for me and preach in tent crusades just like this man."

It seemed practically unbelievable to me. I was from a very poor family. Most of us worked selling newspapers or doing whatever we could to earn some money to provide for the family. I was working at the local store in the produce department for 30c an hour, all of which went to help Mom and the family. I had cardboard in the bottom of my shoes to block up the holes in them and I wore the same shirt with a frayed collar, day in and day out. I thought to myself, "How will I ever travel the world preaching at crusades?!"

Yet, we serve an awesome, amazing God. In due course He would give me the privilege of not only preaching at many tent revivals, but also in stadiums in cities around the world that I had not even heard of. Nothing is impossible with God!

Drafted and sent to the Korean conflict

In 1954 I was a happy, contented young man, living in Fort Worth and attending my home church, Northside Assembly of God, which was located on North Main and Exchange and presided over by Pastor Jacob Filbert. I went along faithfully and was very active in the church, which at that time had over a hundred young people my age.

I lived by myself at Simpson's Room and Board House and had a good job at the local sheet metal factory, Corn Aluminum Awnings. I had not long been promoted to be the manager over my department when one day the shop foreman called me into his office, saying that there was a very important phone call waiting for me.

Wondering who could be calling me at work, I picked up the phone.

"Hello?"

Without ceremony, the voice on the other end responded in monotone:

"The President of the United States and your friends and neighbors have selected you for the Armed Forces. You are to report to the induction office of the military in one week. Do you understand me?"

That was it.

"Yes, I understand," I said and hung up.

The shop foreman laughed and said jokingly, "Hey, who was that – your draft board?"

"Yes, it certainly was," I responded. "And I am leaving in a week!"

His attitude changed and he began to tell me he was sorry, he didn't realize.

"Don't be sorry," I told him. "There's nothing to be sorry about. But I guess I'll be leaving here."

During the next few weeks, change came to my life like a whirlwind. I reported to the induction office in Fort Worth and found myself put on a bus bound for Dallas, Texas. I was there for three days for a physical and lots of paperwork. Then, once I had received my service details, I was put straight onto a plane to fly, for the first time, to Fort Ord in California. I never even had the opportunity to return home for a visit with my family before leaving.

Moving from base to base is part and parcel of army life. I went through the basic training program at Fort Ord and was then sent on to Fort Carson in Colorado. After several weeks there, the next stop was Fort Lee in Virginia, before moving to Fort Lewis, Washington. After just two weeks there I was dispatched to Hawaii – which at that time was classified a foreign country, not a state of the Union. It was from here that I was eventually assigned to a ship and sent to Okinawa, Japan.

Life in the military takes some adjusting to. Orders come from above and the regular soldiers are the last to know anything. You may think you are working to a particular plan and then it changes at a moment's notice and you are heading somewhere else to do something different. I was expecting to be based in Okinawa for some time, but as it was, I got off the ship for twenty-four hours only and then found myself back on the same ship, heading for Yokohama.

We went through a terrible storm en route and – just to complete the biblical imagery – managed to hit a whale, damaging our rudder. We remained in Yokohama for a few days whilst we made repairs to the vessel and then I set off on my last jaunt. After being on that tub for twenty-one days I eventually arrived in Korea, where the army finally seemed to forget about me and left me for the next sixteen months and four days.

In a baffling move that only military minds more advanced than mine could see the logic of, I was assigned to the 82nd Engineers, attached to the 24th Infantry division, and given a job that bore no resemblance to anything the Army had trained me for. What a rude awakening! I had completed several months of training to become a Quartermaster, and now here I was in Korea setting about tackling something far different.

On day one I was taken outside and confronted with a D7 Caterpillar 3T – which for the uninitiated is a huge tractor-type vehicle commonly used as a bulldozer or excavator, with a large blade fitted to the front.

"This is yours," said my Sargent simply.

I was bemused. I walked all the way around it several times before finally asking, somewhat embarrassedly,

"How do you start this thing?"

The Sargent couldn't believe his ears and laughed:

"You mean to say you don't even know how to start it soldier?"

"No sir, I've only seen one from a distance. I was trained to do something totally different than operate one of these!"

I didn't have a clue what I was supposed to be doing, but it didn't take me long to learn. I sat on that machine for the next year. My job was to shift earth and plow roads for the 24th Infantry, cutting passages through the mountains. This work was interrupted periodically by my Sargent yanking me out of my seat and throwing me face down in a ditch whilst enemy fire burst over our heads. Once these mini-crises were over, it was back to shifting earth.

Many a day was spent in miserable weather conditions, sitting in the freezing cold under a torrent of driving rain. Most people's impression of Korea is that of a hot, humid country, but the difference between summer and winter is striking. The winter is bitterly cold, on a par with Alaska, with temperatures measured in minus figures!

During the floods of 1956 I was confined to sitting on that bulldozer for three entire days and nights. Intense, unremitting rain washed away all the vegetation from the mountainsides and we struggled to keep the mountain passes open for the infantry. A river of water and mud was almost submerging the caterpillar tracks of my D7. After such a long period of time in the relentless cold, wind and rain I was sent to a Quonset hut to rest for a few hours. I immediately came down with a very high fever and pneumonia. I was apparently completely disorientated and saying all kinds of weird things.

They had to get me to a MASH outfit, which we called an EVAC hospital, because my temperature continued to soar and I was still delirious. I remember so clearly waking up briefly as I was being carried on the shoulders of my buddies. They placed me on the back of an open Jeep and tied me down with straps so that I wouldn't just roll off on the way! Then came a terrible, bone-jarring journey of several miles to the EVAC. I remember being strapped down, flat on my back, with the rain pounding heavily on my face. I felt as though I was drowning and the journey seemed to take forever.

After the bleak, freezing conditions on the mountain, for the next two weeks I found myself recovering in hospital. I hadn't laid eyes on an American woman for a year or so and suddenly I was surrounded by nurses. Their job was to patch me up and get me back to work – which is exactly what they did – but it was nice while it lasted!

A soldier of the Lord

I took advantage of my time in Korea to learn the local language. By the time I left I could converse in Korean pretty well. I was privileged to have a Korean man assigned to work alongside me as I worked at cutting roadways. He had been an English teacher in High School prior to the Korean conflict, so for several months I benefitted from his patient teaching and every time I needed to say something in Korean he would teach me how to say it. This is still a blessing to me to this day, as I've had many opportunities to have conversations with Koreans over the years.

Besides the language, the Korean conflict taught me one very valuable lesson – how fragile life really is. When you find yourself in the midst of war and see other men die around you – whether they are on your side or not – it brings your view of eternity, and all its implications, into sharp focus. To God, who is no respecter of persons, a life is a life. God loves every person and His desire is that no one should be lost.

I had begun preaching His gospel at fourteen years of age and I looked towards a future filled with serving Him more. Although surrounded by war and conflict, my faith and trust was in God. I have never had a problem looking back and trying to process the many things I experienced in the military, because I always knew that He had called me to His service. He had a mission prepared for me – to send me to many parts of the world to build His Kingdom – and I was intent on fulfilling that mission. I will always be grateful to the pastors and youth leaders of my first church, who were committed to instilling the Word of God in my heart. It served to give my life a firm foundation for what lay ahead.

In 1957 I returned from Korea, just prior to my twenty-first birthday. I continued to serve in the military until

1961 when I was discharged and returned to my home state of Texas. To this day I don't regret the time I spent in the army, because it brought many benefits – not least of which was discipline and endurance – qualities that would serve me well in the mission field. Experiencing different cultures, languages, and ways of life had also awakened me to the need that existed in many parts of the world.

As I started a whole new adventure, I continually gave thanks to God that He had protected and preserved me during this time. I had returned as a soldier of the United States Army, but now I was consumed with being a soldier in God's Army, with a desire to serve Him by serving others. Right after I turned twenty-four I married my wonderful wife, Doris. Just thirty days after our wedding we reopened a church that had been shut down for nearly two years and began our first pastorate and full time ministry. We have just completed our forty-fourth year of "active service". You'll learn more about our adventures in the rest of this book.

CHAPTER 2

Meet Doris

I was born on July 3, 1941, to Willie Alfice and Emma Jewel Baze Stanley in the small town of Italy, Texas. I have one brother, Alfice Leon Stanley, who has been a pastor for many years and is also married to Franklin's sister Shirley.

Both Franklin and I seem to have had church planting in our DNA. My parents, like his, were holding prayer meetings in their home and helping to start churches before I was born. I accepted Jesus as my Savior at the age of seven. Then, when I was eleven, an evangelist called Richard Jeffrey came to First Assembly of God in Alvarado, Texas, to preach at a revival meeting. He spoke about being baptized in the Holy Ghost with the evidence of speaking in tongues. I was ready to have a deeper relationship with God and was keen to receive what He had for me. That night the Lord touched me during an awesome, powerful experience. Many years later, in 1979, Franklin and I were privileged to minister together with Richard Jeffrey in San Jose, Costa Rica. What an honor!

I was just nine when I decided that I wanted to learn to play the piano, after watching Moran Annear, the pianist at our church in Alvarado. I sang in the choir and always made sure that I stood right behind him so that I could watch him play. In those days, when the service started anyone who wanted to sing just walked up onto the platform and took part in the choir. I was always there.

I told my parents that I wanted piano lessons. Money was very hard to come by in those days, but I pestered them until I finally talked them into letting me learn. They were willing to sacrifice the 50c per hour it would cost. I only took lessons for six months. Firstly, that was all my parents could afford. But secondly, my piano teacher could only play by note out of the hymnbook and I liked playing by ear also. Then, one Wednesday night, Brother Annear was sick and there was no one to play the piano, so the pastor said, "Doris, this is your time to fill in." I said okay and went to the piano. I was scared, but I also knew the Holy Spirit would help me. All went well!

When I was around twelve, my parents bought up 10 acres of land on Highway 81 between Alvarado and Grandview, Texas. Over the next two years we all worked hard and helped to build a family home. It felt like a great accomplishment and we were all very excited and happy about it. Then one day, my parents called my brother and me together and told us they felt God was calling our family to pioneer a church in Meridian, some 50 miles away. Both the land and the house would have to be sold in order to raise the money to purchase another plot of land and build a church. We all prayed about it and decided we would do it. The sale of the land and house came to $10,000. That same land was later sold for many thousands of dollars more, since it is now the site of Interstate 35!

One thing I learned, however, is that God always has a plan. We found a new house in Meridian and set about turning it into our new home. At the same time we began to hold prayer meetings there and seek God about His plans for the new church. Shortly afterwards, a man gave us a property, right next door to the Dairy Queen convenience store, that would become the Assembly of God church.

My brother, Alfice, graduated high school in Meridian and answered God's call on his life to pastor the Assembly of God church in Comanche, Texas. I was still in high school at the time. One weekend Alfice invited me to come and spend the weekend with him at his church, and I drove up there in the little Henry J car I had managed to acquire. Little did I know who I would meet that weekend.

The family who had started the church that Alfice was now pastoring had a daughter called Shirley. My brother would later marry her. He said I could stay with Shirley and thought I would enjoy doing so, as she was the church pianist. When I walked into her house that weekend there was a handsome young man sitting in the kitchen with his feet propped up on the table and smoking a cigarette. Shirley introduced me to him as her youngest brother. It was Franklin. Until then I had never even had a boyfriend or been on a date, but at that moment I said to myself, "Wow! I am going to marry him!"

At the same time, I wondered how exactly that could be, since I had set my heart on marrying a preacher and going into the ministry. All I knew about this boy was that he was in the military. He had just returned from a long posting in Korea and was briefly visiting home on leave, before moving to his next posting. He would be there for at least a further two years. Nevertheless, we began to get acquainted and I was having a lovely weekend until he announced that the next day he had to go to Brownwood, "to meet a girl". Shirley and I took him there and as he was getting out of the car, he leaned over and said, "See you baby," kissing me on the cheek. I cried all the way back to Comanche!

Back in Meridian I told my parents about this boy I had met and how I intended to marry him someday. My dad was definitely not happy about this! The next week Franklin showed up at our house. He had come to tell me that the Army was sending him to Alaska for two years. It's funny the things we remember. We had hamburgers that day and Franklin asked for extra onions on his, which I didn't care for. My mother immediately assumed that her and Dad had nothing more to worry about me: "Doris would never marry a man who ate onions!" Mom declared.

Franklin and I wrote to each other for the next two years during his posting in Alaska. I finished high school and went to Bible School for a year, spending most of my spare time involved in leading children's revival meetings and being the pianist for a number of other churches that we were experiencing revival. Meanwhile, my parents resigned their pastorate of the church in Meridian to accept a new position at First Assembly of God church in Moody, Texas.

In the October of 1960 Franklin came home on furlough briefly, with just two more months to go before he was discharged from the Army. He borrowed his Mom's car and came straight over to see me. We just spent time together and talked a lot about the future. It was then that I learned Franklin had begun preaching at the age of fourteen, before he was drafted, and wanted to go into full time ministry as soon as he was discharged. I already knew what my calling was – and it was the same as his. This was exciting!

We sat together on the steps of that little rock church in Moody, chatting away, when Franklin suddenly said,

"I have a question for you."

"What is it?" I replied.

"Are you going to marry me?" he asked. "I need to know now, because I have places to go and things to do!"

It was direct, to say the least! I thought for just a moment and then said, "Yes!"

Franklin went back to Alaska to finish his service and arrived back home at the end of 1960. We were married in Moody at First Assembly on March 10, 1961 by Rev. E. R. Anderson. We lived in Moody for a month before we felt God lead us to go to Graford, Texas, to re-open a church that had been closed for nearly two years. Thus began a brand new chapter in both of our lives and an adventure that is still being written.

Since then Franklin and I have traveled and ministered together across the US and in many other countries around the world. Our theme song has always been, "We have come this far by faith, leaning on the Lord, and we will not turn back now!"

PART ONE

Pioneer Evangelism

CHAPTER 3

A Call to Pioneering Ministry

At twenty-four years old I married Doris Stanley and, just a month later, we moved to Graford, Texas, in an area called Possum Kingdom to re-open a church that had been closed for eighteen months. It was the start of our ministry together. I guess we thought we might be based there a long time before perhaps moving on to pastor other churches in other towns across Texas – but God had other plans.

I still recall, as though it were yesterday, how God spoke to me through the voice of a singer who was conducting the choir in our church. His name was Doug Putnam. Physically he was a very short, very large man – but what a voice! It was beautiful; captivating.

Over the years I've learned that God will speak to us in many different ways. More often than not He speaks through His Word. He also speaks to us through His Holy Spirit who whispers into our hearts. But many times He simply uses other believers to deliver His message to us. This is the wonder of body of Christ at work. So it was that on this Sunday evening, as a choir from a nearby Bible School, ably led by Doug, sang in our church, the voice of the Lord rung out like a thunder clap in my heart. I knew, beyond a shadow of a doubt, that He had spoken.

"You are to resign this church and prepare to leave for South America. You are now being sent."

It came so powerfully that I couldn't remain in my seat. Like the commissioning call that Isaiah experienced when God asked, "Whom shall I send? Who will go?" and he was compelled to reply, "Here I am, send me!" I responded in similar fashion ... with not the faintest idea of what I was actually signing up to!

Nevertheless, the details didn't matter at this precise moment. I was on my feet praising God. He had spoken! Then God's presence enveloped me and I found myself weeping, crying out, "Yes, Lord, I will. I will be obedient to your word and to your calling."

The church we were pastoring was doing well, growing and thriving. We had just purchased a new home and some furniture, plus a new car. We had a good income and we were having the time of our lives settling into our new role when this "divine interruption" came.

A few years earlier I'd sensed that one day, some day, God would call us to be missionaries in some foreign land. Doris and I had even felt to submit an application to our church denomination's missions board. But we never heard back from them and God seemed to be silent on the matter. The call had not come, so nothing had happened. Nevertheless, the feeling had never left me. Now God had spoken, somewhat unexpectedly, but when the message came, it came loud and clear. Surely we were on our way.

Once He has spoken to us, God will usually confirm His word through a number of other sources. Later that night, after the service was over and everyone had gone their separate ways, I spoke to Doris about what had happened. I relayed the message I felt God had spoken to me earlier.

"God has just spoken clearly to me tonight that we are being sent – that we're to leave here and go to South America," I said.

"Yes," Doris responded, "I felt that too!"

We both marveled at God's methods in calling His servants.

Then things got really interesting! The next morning, one of our church deacons, a man by the name of RD Hays, stopped by our house. RD worked in the nearby oil fields as a pumper. He had to go and visit some of the rigs to carry out equipment checks and wanted some company.

"Sure, I can go with you," I told him.

We jumped into his truck and set off and were riding down the road, going from one rig to another, when RD turned and looked at me.

"Pastor, when are you leaving?"

"Leaving?" I responded, surprised. "I don't know what you're talking about."

RD smiled wryly. "Hey Pastor, you're not supposed to lie!" he chuckled.

"Well, I'm not lying," I said, "so tell me what's on your mind."

He told me that he and his wife, Carol, had been praying together following the previous night's service.

"The Lord spoke to us and told us to pray for you, Pastor," he continued, "because you're leaving for South America."

My face must have been a picture of shock and bemused puzzlement. Had I heard God speak to me? Yes, without a doubt. Was I expecting Him to speak to other members of the church about the matter simultaneously? Absolutely not! It had been a little less than twelve hours since the Lord had spoken, yet here was as clear a confirmation as I could have hoped for. I assured RD that we were all hearing clearly from God and that I would be letting people know in due course.

But, there was more to come.

Later that day I received a phone call telling me that one of the older ladies in our church, Sister Vassar, urgently needed to see Doris and I at her home. She was a wonderful ninety-year old lady whose children were missionaries in India. It sounded urgent – "You must go *immediately...*" – so I figured she must be sick or she'd had an accident and fallen or something. We rushed over to her house.

Knocking on the door I was surprised when Sister Vassar opened it herself, looking quite well. Slightly puzzled, we went inside. She didn't bother with any niceties. As was her way, she came right to the point:

"Sit down, young man, I need to talk to you," she began.

"Yes Ma'am," I said respectfully and did as I'd been asked.

"I have been praying for you all day," she told me. Then, continuing the theme that had quickly developed: "God revealed to me that you are going to be leaving here to go to South America as a missionary."

I raised my eyebrows, but said nothing.

"I just wanted to tell you," she continued, "that everything is going to be alright. God has His hand on you. He is going to bless you and use you. Now I want to pray over you."

This dear woman of God laid her hands on my forehead and began to pray God's blessing and anointing on me, stating that the anointing would be upon both Doris and I as we embarked on God's adventure for us on the mission field.

Later, as we left Sister Vassar's house, Doris and I marveled at the awesomeness of God. He had spoken to each of us clearly as individuals, and now He had given two confirmations that were as clear as could be, through two other believers that we highly respected. As if all of this wasn't enough, then came the icing on the cake.

Later that week I received a phone call from a member of the Mission's Board for our church denomination, based in Springfield, Missouri. Delmar Guynes was the Secretary of the Board and he told me that he wanted to come and visit our town and spend at least three days with us to talk about the possibility of us becoming missionaries for the organization. I was ecstatic.

"Yes sir," I said, "We would love to talk with you."

A date was set and Mr. Guynes came almost immediately, staying in our home. He told us that he had only recently taken over the post of Secretary and had been busy familiarizing himself with his new role. Settling into his new office, he had stumbled across the application that Doris and I had submitted some four years earlier. It was languishing in the bottom drawer of a dusty filing cabinet – along with some long forgotten mildewed sandwiches! God had touched this man's heart and he'd felt compelled to contact us.

"I can't quite explain this," he said, "so I felt I had to come and see you in person. I was setting about arranging my office the way I wanted it when I found your application. I just *knew* I had to come and visit with you. I want you to come and meet with the Mission Board and I will help you fulfill your calling become missionaries."

Seven months later, with the blessing of the board, we were all packed up and leaving for language school to study Spanish.

That was forty-five years ago and we are still going strong! God is still speaking to us, still opening doors and, more importantly, still using us to plant churches and see more and more people brought into His Kingdom. Every day we thank Him for good health and His supernatural power to accomplish all He has set before us.

What is a pioneer evangelist?

As exciting as it was to be called by God and to have that calling confirmed through many respected, trusted people, this was really just the beginning of the story. The real adventure began when we launched out in faith and began to follow where God led us.

I have often been asked the question, "What exactly is a pioneer evangelist?" by people trying to understand what it is that we do. I want to take some time to explain the mission and the method.

Pioneer evangelism has also been called "missionary evangelism" and "new church evangelism" and today remains a unique type of ministry, which very few people operate in. Rather than trying to revive a failing church in an area where there is already a Christian presence, or planting a new church in an area near other established churches (which invariably attracts a certain amount of "transfer growth" as believers who are dissatisfied with their own church move to join you), pioneer evangelism seeks to plant where there is no church.

We go to places where there is no Christian presence and no, or very few, churches. We find a strategic city or town in that place in which we base ourselves, and then set up home as if we are going to live there forever. Then we begin to pray over the city/town and ask for God's direction. We ask Him to show us the right location in which to establish a new church. Sometimes this process takes a few days, sometimes a few weeks, but eventually we know when we have found the location that God desires by a strong sense of witness from the Holy Spirit.

What happens after this is described in more detail in the following chapters, but for now let me say this: it requires us to develop a radical trust and dependency on God; a willingness to launch out in obedience to Him, believing that God will make a way to supply all our needs.

Much like Abraham, who "*...set out, not knowing where he was going*" (Hebrews 11:8 NKJV), we went and we trusted in the word we had received that God would "have His hand upon us".

He did not let us down!

CHAPTER 4

Discovering God's Model For Pioneer Evangelism

I knew without a shadow of doubt that God had called me and Doris to be pioneering missionaries. We were obedient to that call and committed to following wherever God led us. We had resigned the pastorate of our church and were now traveling thousands of miles throughout our state of Texas, ministering in many churches and raising the thousands of dollars wc would need to fund ourselves to live in a foreign country for the next several years.

Whilst living and pastoring in Possum Kingdom we had added two further members to the Burns clan – our daughters Wynelle and Sharon. When it was time to go, we sold our furniture, our car and practically everything we owned, packed up our children and our personal belongings and left for Latin America. Our ultimate destination was the city of Cartagena in Colombia, South America, but we initially we spent time learning Spanish at a language school in Guadalajara, Mexico, before moving to our designated mission field. We had secured a ready-furnished house where we would live

29

and we were very excited. This would be home for the next few years.

Two weeks after we arrived we started a crusade in a place called Villate. The plan was to set up and preach the gospel, and pioneer our first church in Latin America with the people who got saved. We had assistance from a veteran missionary named Dave Williams, who had already made preparations and was ready to help us start the crusade when we arrived. Dave had heard that our calling was pioneer evangelism and he was excited to meet us. We were happy because here was a man who had lived in the area for several years, and who knew the culture and language as well as any native. After concluding our preaching crusade, Dave and I agreed to combine our finances to help build a church in that part of the town.

We continued the way we had begun. We immediately started another crusade in another part of the town with the purpose of pioneering a second church. Not long after that Dave had to leave the country for several months and so Doris and I continued doing evangelism and starting new churches. During our first full year on the mission field we were able to establish six churches and set them in order, with designated pastors, Sunday school superintendents and a Board of Trustees.

Others told us that what we were doing was the most awesome thing any new missionary could do and commended us for being able to establish so many churches in such a short space of time – but something was missing. I wasn't as excited or happy about the results as everyone else seemed to be, because after a few months, when I returned to see how those churches were getting along, they were only about half as strong as they were when we'd left them. Attendance was down, finances were down, and the pastors were having a hard time keeping going on such a low income. I was confused. I didn't understand what the problem was, but I knew that something was not right.

I stopped to examine what we were doing. I was running each crusade for about two or three weeks, preaching the gospel and seeing people saved. Immediately following that I initiated a building program, quickly moving on to create a "house of God" for these new believers. Once the governance structure was set in place, with appropriate leaders, I moved on to a new area and began a new crusade. It all seemed fairly logical.

I talked things over with Doris. "It's not working," I told her. "I feel as though I'm planting churches like I would if we were in the US – but this is not the US. These people have not heard the gospel over and over again like we have in America. So we've got to find out what we are doing wrong."

We agreed together that I would take time out to seek the Lord for the answer. I would check into a local hotel and stay there for as many days as it took for me to hear from God and to understand His plan for pioneering indigenous churches. I knew I had to go on my own, be alone with God, and to fast, pray and seek His direction and guidance. I was burning with the desire to carry out the vision He had planted in my heart.

I found a hotel in Barranquilla called El Prado. I took only my Bible and a notebook and pen. I checked in with no idea of exactly how long I was going to stay there. I had told Doris that she was to be the only person who knew where I was. I was determined that no one else should know, because I didn't want to be disturbed. I had to be alone with God and hear from Him. "I'll let you know when it's time to join me!" I told her and off I went.

I got settled in the hotel and began to walk the floor of my room. I can picture it now. Committed to fasting and praying I began to pace up and down and pray. I was determined to not eating a thing until I heard from God. The minutes turned into hours – many hours! – and I continued to pace. At times I would stop and read particular scriptures over and over. My notebook and pen were laid out ready to start writing as soon as God began to speak, but He didn't speak. Day one passed – nothing. Day two passed – nothing. Now I was approaching the end of day three and still I had heard nothing!

By now I was a little desperate. That third night I knelt down beside my bed, placing my Bible and notebook in front of me and started to read more of God's Word. I guess I was pretty exhausted because after a short while I fell asleep. This was no nap, but a deep sleep. I don't know how long I stayed in that position, but I eventually awoke, with my Bible still open at the same page in front of me.

Now God spoke to me. Revelation came in a flood and I began to write. It was almost as though God was standing in front of me dictating the words. I scribbled it all down as fast as I could. Minutes later I had God's guidance on how to do pioneer evangelism – His way. This was 1972. Since then, I have never stopped doing it the way He taught me and I'm still doing the last thing He told me to do!

What God spoke to me distilled down into two profound principles – both of which meant that I had to do things differently from the way I'd been doing them.

First, God told me that I was not to go into a town or area and preach for two or three weeks then build a building. Instead, it had to be an extended crusade – one that lasted three or four months, maybe even six months – preaching every night until there was a sizeable congregation of new believers. This way we would plant a church with enough people for it to be self-supporting. There would be enough finances coming in to support a full time pastor, who could then look after the people.

Second, God instructed me to *build on demand*. In other words, I was not to rush to construct a building and then work to try and fill it. Instead, I was to focus on building the real church – the people – and then, when demand dictated, we would construct a building to create a permanent home for the church, which already existed.

This is what we began to do, with predictably different and considerably better results. In this way, Doris and I have pioneered over fifty churches. Some three hundred more churches have been started as church plants from those churches, with pastors continuing with the same vision, teaching, training and discipling their people to do the same.

We will continue a crusade until we feel the Holy Spirit say it is time to stop. Sometimes it has been necessary to continue for up to seven months. On one occasion we continued for a whole fifteen months because we were planting in a particularly spiritually hard place. Invariably, God would speak to us about where and when to start a crusade, but He allowed us to discern when it was time to move on, saying, "You will know when it is time to build."

Each time the witness of the Holy Spirit would come and we would know it was time for us to leave the church that had been established and move to the next location God had prepared for us. This might be in the same city, or the next city, or the same country, or a different country! This is what makes this life so exciting and unpredictable.

I remain so grateful to God that He gave me a specific plan for our type of ministry. Today there are churches that have been established with members running into the thousands, which are vibrant and thriving, busy planting other churches. The pastors are well compensated and have the necessary support to raise their families and have their own homes. This is the work of God. There is provision in all that we do because God is alive! And still, there is so much more to be done, according to God's will and purpose.

* * *

On one occasion I was invited to attend a small conference in Springfield, Missouri, with several other missionaries who were doing the same type of ministry as us. Some of them were based in Chile, some in Argentina and Panama, and others in Africa. There were only about six couples in all because there are not too many people committed to this kind of pioneering ministry. It is a challenge to go into a strange city, set up and preach the gospel day in and day out for months, gradually building a congregation and eventually establishing a church. To grow a church to the point where it is a strong, vibrant work of God takes a specially dedicated person and family.

At this conference, each of us took turns to talk about how we had heard from God and been directed by Him to set about what we were doing. It was an immense privilege to sit among a few missionaries who were carrying out new church evangelism the same way that Doris and I were. The really miraculous part was that we all had almost identical stories to tell. God had instructed each one of us to carry out extended crusades before we ever thought of constructing a building, and to do so only on demand. We were to follow this pattern over and over. God was with each of us and the churches were successful. They were successful simply because we were obeying God and doing it His way.

I learned one further lesson from this discussion. Each of us had to disregard whatever model of church planting we had been taught in our homeland and seek God to discover His will for the places He was sending us to. Our overall method was absolutely identical. The only slight differences between each set of missionaries' way of working arose from minor cultural differences – challenges that were specific to the context in which we found ourselves, peculiar to that nation.

Over the years I have witnessed many church organizations seek to acquire a building and then attempt to fill it. I still believe what God told me, that the opposite approach is what is needed. I learned that the former way makes weak churches with people who have a low sense of belonging. They have joined a church – they haven't made a church. Instead of being vitally involved from the beginning, part of the fabric of the church, they are "invited" to get involved. But they don't have the same sense of ownership.

Instead we look to build "the church – the people", who then help to build "the church – the building". People have to invest of themselves into that eventual building. Then it will be a successful work.

As far as I am concerned, all of these churches are not ours, but His, the Lord's. Our role is just to be obedient to our call and do what we are told to do. The plan came from the throne room of God, so it works, over and over again. I give all the praise, glory and honor to Him!

I invite you to accept and apply this same challenge to your own life. Hear what God is saying to you personally, and then go and do what He says!

CHAPTER 5

One By One – Practical Pioneering

The joys and blessings of the process of church planting begin with a Good News Crusade. This is simply what it sounds like – we hold a series of meetings and share the simple, wonderful, profound and powerful truths of the gospel of Jesus Christ. We share the good news that Jesus came to set us free from the power of sin and death through the free gift of God's grace and mercy, and to transform our lives for all eternity.

Is it all joy and miracles? No – a vast amount of planning and preparation work must take place before we ever stand on a platform and begin to preach. Let me use the example of a city in Mexico where God called us to pioneer to illustrate the process of practical pioneering.

Matamoros is a city in the northeastern state of Tamaulipas, located on the southern bank of the mighty Rio Grande, which separates it from Brownsville, Texas, across the water. Picture a city of some 500,000 inhabitants – an eclectic mix of the wealthy, the middle class and the poverty stricken. There are no gospel radio programs aired, there is no preaching or singing, no gospel television programs. The people have no one who is sharing the good news of Jesus with them. No one is telling them that there is a God who loves them; who can help to solve their problems; save them from a life of sin and desperation. They have little concept of a God who can heal their diseases. So who can they turn to?

We arrive in the city and find our accommodation. Almost immediately we begin the work of letting the local population know that an event will soon take place. It is not unlike a marketing campaign. Advertisements are produced, handbills printed ready to be given out, gospel tracts created or bought in for distribution. Then there are supplies of Bibles acquired, ready to be given away. Next we arrange radio spot announcements, sharing the news that in the city district of Enrique Cardenas, a Good News Crusade is about to take place. These continue throughout the length of the crusade, inviting more and more people to come and see what is happening.

The announcements are simple and direct, saying, "Jesus Christ is the answer to all your problems. He saves, He heals and He delivers and sets the captive free. The Good News is that He loves you, He cares for you and He will change your life completely."

Prior to the crusade we will have spent many days finding an empty lot somewhere in the city that is suitable for hosting the crusade and, eventually, building a church on. Practically, this means a lot of paperwork. Signing contracts, obtaining permits. Now the hands-on, heavy part of the work begins. The lot has to be cleared and cleaned; a platform has to be constructed; lighting is erected; a sound system is put in place. Once the crusade site is prepared, then the local area is canvassed, with people knocking on doors, giving out leaflets and inviting people to come to a life-changing experience.

Eventually we are ready. How many people will show up on the first night? Sometimes it is twenty-five or thirty; sometimes it is hundreds. It is impossible to predict. We trust that through the work we have done prior to the first meeting, God has touched and prepared the hearts of many to come and meet with Him. The Holy Spirit has been prompting those whose hearts are ready to heard the Good News to come to the crusade. We have done our part, the rest is in the Lord's hands. We trust Him to do what He wants to do.

* * *

On the first night we look up and see many hungry souls coming to see what is going on – people desperate for change in their lives. On the first night in Matamoros around seven hundred people flood into the lot – what a thrill!

Music and singing start the meeting. We sing a chorus in Mexican, *Hay poder en la sangre* – "There is power in the blood". When the singing ends, I greet and welcome the people, who call me Francisco Alonzo, rather than Franklin. I announce that the theme of this crusade is based on the verse from Romans 10:17: *"Faith comes by hearing and hearing by the Word of God."* After this comes fifteen minutes of preaching the word. I tell the people about Jesus Christ and His power to save, heal and change lives. The people listen intently, some weeping as they understand, for the first time, the reality of a God who loves them, cares for them, and who is present and able to touch their lives.

A young man of around twenty makes his way to the front of the meeting. I discover that his name is Jesus Manuel. He is lost in sin and cannot see any hope or future for his life. His life is defined by a dependency on drugs and alcohol to numb the pain of his, as he sees it, pointless existence. He thinks that there is no one in the world who cares whether he lives or dies. But he is wrong! The good news is that Jesus Christ loves him, cares for him and wants to transform his life. We pray with him and the Holy Spirit touches his heart. He sobs and asks God for forgiveness.

Then suddenly, his face breaks into a smile. Peace floods his being and is evident on his face. Christ has entered his heart and changed his life. He leaves the meeting a different man and comes back again night after night. God continues to touch and transform this young man. One night he is healed of broken ribs. Another night he has a powerful experience with the Lord and is baptized in the Holy Spirit. He himself begins to share the good news of how Jesus can transform lives, all over Matamoros.

On another night, Doris shares her own testimony of how God healed her from cancer and diseased kidneys (you can read more about this in a later chapter). A young girl comes forward in response. Her name is Laura Puente and she is nineteen years old. She has received the sad news from her doctor that she has terminal cancer. Humanly speaking, there is no hope for her. But after hearing the good news that Jesus Christ also heals, she believes for a miracle and asks us to pray. We pray for her! She leaves the meeting and we don't see her again for a week or so. But then she returns and comes to tell us, all smiles and joy, that Jesus Christ has made her whole. God has performed a miracle for her and her doctor, amazed and perplexed, has given her a clean bill of health. What an incredible privilege it is to be able to share the good news that Jesus saves, heals and delivers!

During a typical crusade we will minister every night, seven nights per week. This will continue for as long as God tells us, but typically for three to four months according to the model He imparted to us. It will continue longer if that is what it takes. Then, when a "church" has been gathered and leaders identified and anointed by God, we turn to constructing a building to house this new group of believers.

The Bible shows us that the Apostle Paul used this exact method to pioneer new churches. First he went where God led him. Once he had arrived he began to preach the gospel (Acts 19:8). Then he trusted God to perform miracles and transform people's lives, ushering them into the Kingdom (Acts 19:11). He also began to gather together a leadership group and gave them special attention, helping to disciple them (Acts 19:10). When he moved on, he would leave behind a specific leader who he had prayed for and appointed as pastor. Paul didn't start churches by going looking for a building – he would simply start an outreach for the lost. After that the church simply grew, organically as new believers witnessed to others.

When a crusade ends and a new church is established we know that soon we will be moving on to a new location where God is calling us, where we will do it all over again. But it is important that – as the Lord taught us – we don't do so prematurely. We need to remain and keep building until the church is fully birthed by the Holy Spirit. We need to know that it is firmly established and will continue to grow and thrive in the future. We continue until the church is flourishing independently, with a good pastor in place and enough finances to continue the work. Our aim is an indigenous church that is self-supporting and self-governing.

For more than forty years Doris and I, and our children, have traveled through many countries, repeating the model that God taught us. Sometimes we have put up tents, sometimes preached in the open air, and in other places we've needed to rent buildings. Many times God has so poured out His grace and blessings that we have been able to establish more than one church in a location – sometimes up to five. We leave and go to the next place, but the churches and pastors continue with the same vision. Many of the churches we have planted have themselves planted dozens of other churches. One life touches another life, by the help and grace of God.

Of course, this type of ministry does not simply happen without opposition. I have sat and talked with other missionary evangelists who have traveled throughout the world doing this same type of ministry and compared stories. The amazing victories of the gospel are always accompanied by dangers. There are those who react with strong opposition to the word of God being preached. Sometimes the weather is a hindrance as well as the people! So we need to apply dedication, commitment and perseverance, ministering night after night until another church is established.

Today in Enrique Cardenas, Matamoros, Mexico, stands a beautiful church that seats hundreds of people, and the building is filled as the pastor continues to run regular crusades. Miracles are still happening there. The good news is: one more church has been planted.

CHAPTER 6

"Ask of Me..."

Cartagena is a sleepy port on the Caribbean coast of northern Colombia. It was once known as the glory of the Spanish Main and the entryway through which the Conquistadores flooded in to loot the treasures of the highly developed, gold-rich Inca empire. From Cartagena, heavily laden Spanish galleons sailed back to the motherland with their spoils.

Cartagena became a magnet for buccaneers and pirates alike and the city was subjected to repeated sackings, but managed to rise above this to become a center of legitimate trade in the region. Vivacious and full of life, Cartagena became the first province of New Granada to revolt against the Crown in 1810 and by 1815 had declared its independence from Spain, earning the title, "The Heroic City".

Now, the former glory that caused Cartagena to be called "Queen of the Caribbean" has faded without trace. Beyond the high-rise apartment buildings, on the salty bog land of Chambacu, lies one of Colombia's worst slums. Thousands of desperate, poverty-ridden families occupy a vast area – a chaotic sprawl of favela-style tin roofs and makeshift dwellings, with rubbish littering the muddy streets and raw sewage running like streams.

We entered this city, which in the January of 1972 had a population of around 320,000, to pioneer a church and were confronted by the massive scale of the need and deprivation. It would have been easy to quickly become discouraged in such a place, but as always, we followed God's simple plan and made a start.

Going door-to-door and distributing gospel tracts produced by the ministry *Light For The Lost*, we began to discover a few believers who already lived in the slums. At other houses, the occupants were open and hungry to receive, and we were able to lead them to Christ on the spot. From this small beginning we felt God prompting us to start services in various homes throughout the city. We did this and began to teach the Bible, training new Christians to be counselors; ready for the citywide crusade we were planning.

We began to look for a location for our crusade and discovered that among the civic leaders, opposition was strong. At first they dismissed the idea out of hand. "What a ridiculous plan, to hold a gospel crusade – the people will never come to such a meeting!" we were told. Others shared with us that in Cartagena there was a spiritual hardness of heart; people refused to listen to the gospel. "This city is nearly 500 years old," they said. "They have never heard the gospel preached in this way, and they are not going to start now!"

None of this phased me, because I knew that despite their pessimism, the gospel was being preached all around the world and, in spite of intense opposition, was still full of power! I prayed about it and asked for the Lord's direction. God said just one thing to me:

"Find the largest place this city has to offer to host the crusade."

It seemed that not only was God going to make a way for the crusade to happen, despite all the negativity and opposition, He was going to do so in a way that would grab everyone's attention!

I didn't know a great deal about the city and what facilities it had to offer, so I began to search around and ask about the largest venues. Finally, I went to the mayor's office and talked to the mayor's secretary. This lady told me, once again, that the local authorities would not approve permission for any kind of Christian rally in their city. I was wasting their time. I should go away!

I went away, but I came back again. I persevered. I went back to the mayor's office again and again, knocking on their door, persisting in telling them what God had spoken to me about – that the Lord wanted to pay a visit to Cartagena.

Finally, they conceded that there was a theater in the city that could seat some 5,000 people. Each year, around February time, it was used to host an annual movie festival and many famous directors and movie stars would gather from around the world to present and promote their new films.

When I asked for something larger than this, the staff of the mayor's office burst out laughing. Movie stars from all over the world had appeared at the theater and it had never been more than half full. How on earth did I think I could attract a larger crowd?

I persisted and asked them if there was, in fact, a larger venue in the city. There was – a soccer stadium that could seat up to 15,000 people – but it had never been used to host any kind of religious meeting before and it was unlikely that we could get permission to use it. There was another problem too – the stadium had no electricity, so there was no power to support a PA system or lighting.

This might sound extraordinary now, but in the early 70s in South America, electricity was an expensive commodity. Therefore, all soccer games were played during the early afternoon, at about 2.00pm – thus avoiding the need for powered floodlights. Even ordinary people in their homes struggled to afford to pay for electricity. The utilities bills were tremendously high and electrical power was a luxury few could afford.

I took all of this information to God in prayer and sought Him for an answer. After all, He had explicitly instructed me to seek out the largest venue in the city, so I knew He must have something in mind. He said to me, very simply, "Ask of me..."

The Bible is very clear about asking God to meet our needs. Jesus said,

"And whatever you ask in My name, that I will do, that the Father may be glorified in the Son. If you ask anything in My name, I will do it." (John 14:13-14).

Again, Jesus says in John 15:7,

"If you abide in Me, and My words abide in you, you will ask what you desire, and it shall be done for you."

And 1 John 5:14 confirms that,

"This is the confidence that we have in Him, that if we ask anything according to His will, He hears us."

I said to the Lord, "I have found the largest place in the city, but there is no way for us to have it."

"Ask of me..." God replied.

With this, I returned to the mayor's office and told them, "We want to apply for permission use the stadium for our crusade."

After more pessimism, they agreed to process my application, saying, "Okay, but we don't know what you can do with it, because there is no electricity."

In due course, I received the permits we needed to use the stadium. We had overcome the first obstacle. I'm sure they were all laughing about it, since we planned to hold our crusade meetings at 7.30pm each evening – with no power, and therefore in the pitch black!

Next I spoke to the Lord about the power situation. I'm sure you can guess what His answer was! So I went back to the city office and told them,

"I want you to wire the stadium with electricity and I will pay the bill for it."

I had absolutely no money to do so, and I wasn't on some kind of ego trip – I had just gone to the Lord and He had said, "Ask of me and I will give it to you." I admit to responding to the Lord by saying, "I hope you know what you are doing Lord, because I'm just following instructions!"

The local pastors of the city arranged the workforce and they began chiseling through the concrete to embed the electricity cabling and install transformers. We built a platform in the middle of the field and ran the power out to it. Amazingly, they told us, "You can settle the bill for this when you have finished using the stadium – however long that is."

When I stopped by the office to pick up the final paperwork, however, the permit secretary couldn't help but have one last dig at me. *"Usted esta loco,"* she grumbled, handing over the documents. In other words, you are crazy!

"Why am I crazy?" I asked.

She told me, "You are going to look mighty ridiculous in that stadium with ten or fifteen people listening to you preach – because no one is going to go out there!"

"Maybe God knows that we need lots of room?" I said.

By the February of 1973 we were ready to begin our crusade. We had all the permits we needed and the stadium had been wired for power. To the utter amazement of the brazen skeptics, on the first night 5,000 people turned up. By the end of the week the place was full to capacity, with 15,000 people and still more pushing to get in. Every night dozens of miracles took place. People who were deaf, dumb, blind or crippled were miraculously healed. Some 3,000 people were saved during the first week alone.

God can reach anyone

I will tell some of the stories of the people whose lives were touched in the next chapter, but for now I want to relate the story of one particular man. It underlines the amazing truth that God can and will reach anyone. It also reminds me of how God can use simple things – such as the literature we distribute before a crusade – to work in a person's life.

Each tract we give out describes God's plan of salvation and has the address of our crusade stamped on the back so that people can find us. In poor areas such as this, many people cannot read, but they can nearly all recognize and locate an address. Someone had found one of our tracts and thrown it into a trash can. Later a young man named Niebles would discover it.

Niebles was privileged in that he had received a good education, but his life had gone off the rails. He was mainlining hard drugs and his life had fallen apart. He had basically lost everything he owned. Physically he was in very poor condition: he only had the clothes he was standing up in, so he never changed, and had vomited on himself many times after using drugs. He never bathed. He never combed his hair. He was completely fouled up. The only way he could get food was to rummage through the city's garbage cans in back alleys, scavenging for anything remotely edible.

One day, as he was searching for food amongst the garbage, he found one of our pieces of literature in Spanish. He began to read: "Remember, when you are up against the ropes, Jesus saves."

He sat down on the curb with his back up against the trash can and continued to read through blurry eyes. As he did so, the word of God began to touch his life. He noticed the address on the back of the leaflet and decided he would make his way to the crusade.

I am so glad to report that on that very night, Jesus met with Niebles powerfully. He was wonderfully delivered and God set him free from his addiction to drugs and alcohol. Jesus saved him and completely transformed his life, rescuing him from the gutter.

Niebles would later share with us that while he was searching for food for his body, he discovered the spiritual food that would change his life. When we eventually started our second church in Cartagena, Niebles became the pastor. Praise God! What an outstanding miracle!

Our Father God encourages us to come boldly before His throne of grace and ask for all that we need. It is His delight to hear the prayers of His children and give them what they are asking for. Always ask in prayer, expectant that God will meet your need!

CHAPTER 7

Growing in faith

A Colombian poet once wrote of Cartagena, *"Ciudad triste, ayer reina de la mar."* It means, "Sad city, yesterday's queen of the sea." When we found ourselves directed to this city by God, however, we were not ready to write, "the glory has departed" over one of Colombia's great cities. Instead we wanted to ask God to visit Cartagena. This is the heart of pioneer evangelism. We go into cities with literature, gathering and training believers, conducting crusades, training pastors and establishing churches – all with the help of the Holy Spirit's power – and we delight in seeing God visit places that have little or no expectancy of seeing an outbreak of His presence.

So it was that we found ourselves in the city's soccer stadium, looking to see what God would accomplish for His glory. On the first night, 5,000 people arrived to hear the word of God, confounding the skeptics and naysayers. By the end of the first week, the stadium was filled to capacity with 15,000 people. We began with the usual chorus, *There is Power in the Blood.* Soon, all 15,000 were clapping their hands and singing along, *"Hay poder, poder, sin igual poder..."*

Then we noticed that the stadium was actually trembling. The intensity of 15,000 people, all singing together under the anointing of the Holy Spirit, all clapping and stamping their feet, was causing the stadium to shake – so much that one end of the structure was beginning to crack and we saw clouds of concrete dust floating upwards as parts of the structure strained and crumbled. Alarmed, the local officials asked us to begin inviting people to stand on the playing field itself, to relieve the pressure on the stadium infrastructure.

Gratifyingly, one of these was the lady who laughed, predicting we would be rattling around inside the vast stadium with ten or fifteen people. God has a sense of humor! When God says to us, "Ask of me" and we ask, He answers – and He invariably gives us immeasurably more than we can ask or imagine, because He is an abundant giver. God delights in us asking Him to fulfill His will, so we can be sure that if we ask Him for lost souls, He is going to give them.

Night after night we experienced tremendous blessings from God as He performed miracle after miracle. Between three and five hundred people came forward each night to respond to the call for salvation. Such was the response that we needed a virtual army of counselors to pray with those coming forward. The presence of God was so real and tangible – people we literally climbing over one another to get to the front and bathe in His presence.

We had our dear friend, Pastor Eulogio Rivero working alongside us, helping to run the crusade. One night, before I got up to preach, Eulogio pulled me to one side and said he had to tell me something. The city officials had sent a reporter from the main newspaper to report on the crusade and write a story. The man said he must talk to me before I preached. He was standing just off the edge of the platform, so I went over to speak with him. I could see he had a notebook and pencil in his hand.

I greeted him. He responded rather coldly and got straight to the point.

"I am the editor of the newspaper in this city," he informed me. "I've come to write a story on what is happening at this stadium. I believe what's going on here is of the devil and you are a hypocrite."

I didn't know what evidence he had to call me a hypocrite, but I guessed he was just trying to provoke me.

"I am going to have you driven out of this city," he continued icily. "I will expose you for the fraud you are tomorrow, to the entire population. It will be on the front page. This will be your last service."

Inside I prayed and asked God how I should respond. I felt His presence envelope me and I found myself inviting the man onto the platform.

"My friend, don't go and sit out there in the bleachers with the rest of the people," I told him. "Please stand right here in the corner of the platform and write down every word I say. Write down everything that happens from now till the end of the service and don't you miss a trick, brother. Put it all in your story!"

"Oh, I will!" he responded evenly.

After this exchange, I actually forgot about him standing at the edge of the platform, because I became engrossed in God's presence and focused on the task at hand. I concentrated on preaching God's word and then opened up the evening for ministry.

The first person we prayed for was an elderly blind lady. She had been blind for many years, since her early childhood. As we prayed she looked up and exclaimed that she could see the lights across the top of the platform. We continued to pray and then she cried out that she could see everyone. Jesus had opened her eyes.

The second person we prayed for was a boy of around ten or eleven. He was deaf and mute. He had been born this way and had neither heard nor spoken a word his entire life. We prayed and after a short time a huge smile spread across his face. He grinned from ear to ear and I knew something had happened. I looked at him and thought, "Well, I guess this boy doesn't know Spanish from English, or Chinese for that matter, so I'll ask him to say something." I looked into his eyes and said, "Say Jesus." He beamed back at me, took the microphone out of my hand and yelled into it: "JESUS!". The first word he ever uttered was Jesus!

Behind this little boy came a man with his two sons. His boys were literally holding him upright. He walked with a pair of crutches, but was in such poor condition that he also needed his sons to brace him, because his legs simply wouldn't support him. We prayed for him. Within a couple of minutes that man was standing bolt upright and thrusting his now redundant crutches into my hands. Then he took off, running round and round as fast as he could, before coming back to stand in front of me grinning. God had healed his legs and given him strength. What a miracle!

We went on praying for people throughout the night. While this was happening, God had been working another miracle. I looked across and saw the newspaper editor, still standing in the corner of the stage. I walked over to him and couldn't help glancing at his notebook. I saw that he had not written down one single word. We looked at each other.

"You haven't written anything down," I stated. He ignored this comment.

"Do you know who that first woman was?" he asked.

"No, I've never seen her before," I answered.

"That is my aunt," he told me. "She has been blind ever since I have known her."

"The Lord has healed her!" I told him.

"I know," he said. Then, "Do you know the little boy you prayed for, after the lady?"

I told him I didn't.

"He is my nephew," he told me. "He has been deaf and mute from birth."

Then, unbelievably, he continued: "The third person you prayed for – the man on crutches – he is my cousin."

"Are you related to everyone here?" I asked, half joking.

"Only those three, that I know of," he responded with a smile. Astonishingly, God had brought, out of a crowd of 15,000 people, three in succession who were all related to this man. His demeanor suddenly changed. His eyes welled up and tears began to run down his cheeks. "Tell me," he said. "How does a person accept this Jesus?"

"Just invite Him into your heart," I said softly. And right there and then, he raised both hands in the air and invited Jesus to be his Lord and Savior.

The next day there was indeed a big story on the front page of the city newspaper. But it wasn't the story that this man had set out to write. The editor wrote,

"Yesterday I went to the stadium, Pedro de Heredia, and there I saw miracle after miracle. Blind eyes were opened, deaf ears were unstopped, the lame walked...". He went on to tell more about the miracles he had seen. He closed his editorial with a line that money couldn't buy from any newspaper editor: "If you don't believe it, go and see for yourself!"

Numerous people did just that, including many of his newspaper colleagues. The next evening, another man showed up and asked to speak to me, announcing himself as the deputy editor of the newspaper. "The editor was here last night," he said.

"Yes," I confirmed.

"He told me something happened to him and he sent me to get the story."

I understood where this was going, so I said to the man, "Well you stand right beside me, here on the platform, and don't move." I had him stand in the exact same spot as his boss. I preached and later, as people came forward to receive Jesus, and as God performed many miracles, I looked across to see the deputy editor with his hands raised and his face lifted towards the sky. He was saying the name of Jesus, over and over. That night he too was saved.

Another miracle

In due course the crusade came to an end and we set about establishing a church in the city. As promised I returned to the mayor's office. The officials greeted me warmly this time, and then asked, "Why did you come here today?"

"I've come to pay the bill for wiring the stadium," I told them, "and to pay the electricity bill for all the power we used."

The mayor himself came out to speak to me and asked, "You have had a good time here?"

"Yes," I said.

"So what can I do for you?"

"I've just come to pay the bill like I said I would," I told him, a bit puzzled.

"This has been good for our city," the mayor told me. "Last night we had a city council meeting and everyone voted to pay for the cost of the work and the electricity bill. You do not owe us anything."

"What about the cost of hiring the stadium," I asked, not quite believing my ears. "I was told that would be expensive."

"We voted to pay that also," he told me.

How like the Lord. He said "Ask of me" and then did more than I could imagine!

After this amazing experience we moved from the soccer stadium to a location in the very heart of the city where we built a new church building. On the Sunday that the building was dedicated, several miracles occurred.

One man who attended had not spoken a word or taken a step for thirty-eight years. A spinal injury at the age of seven had left him helpless. As we prayed for him the Lord reminded me of the miracle recorded in Acts 3. Like Peter, I said, "In the name of Jesus, rise up and walk." The man jumped up immediately. Then he began jumping up and down. Then he took off and ran around the building. Over and over he repeated the name of Jesus. When I shouted, "Hallelujah" he echoed my praise shouting, "Hallelujah, hallelujah, hallelujah!"

I have said that we will stay where God puts us until a church is fully birthed and it is time for us to move on. We ended up staying for two years in Cartagena and planting four churches. Out of those four churches, twelve further churches were planted. The churches in Cartagena have continued to grow and today there are many churches with hundreds of people in attendance at each. Praise God for His goodness.

CHAPTER 8

Called To Be A Missionary?

Do you believe that God has a sense of humor? I do. It helps to know this if you plan to live the life of a pioneer evangelist. It also helps if you have one too!

One time, Doris and I had arrived in the country of Costa Rica for the purpose of pioneering a new church. Our first task would be to find an appropriate piece of land and prepare to hold an open-air crusade. Open-air because, at that time, we didn't possess a tent, and in any case we were in a warm enough climate.

We began to get acquainted with the city and its layout and we prayed for God's direction to guide us to a place suitable for an outdoor crusade. After several days we found a place that would work, located right in the gateway to the city. But, though it was a nice piece of real estate, there was really no good or, let's say, *easy* way to get to it from the road. To make it a suitable site for the crusade would necessitate creating proper access to the site, cutting down the immensely high grass, picking up all the trash and clearing an area large enough to host our meetings.

So we made a start. You may wonder why we didn't have people around us who could carry out these manual tasks. Well, when you go into a new country to begin a pioneer work, it means just that. You are alone; you have no help. At that point there is no church, so there is no team of willing helpers to do the jobs that need to be done. It's just you and your family!

Doris and I worked hard for a month, preparing the location. This meant a great deal of hard work: shifting garbage; digging holes and placing 4x4 timbers in the ground to mark out the site; running electrical wiring around for lighting. It also meant constructing a platform that would be large enough to carry all PA equipment and accommodate musical instruments, so that we could have music at our events.

It was tough work, but after a month we were ready for our crusade to begin. We had done our preparation work and advertised the meetings to the city, and we were excited to begin ministering to the people. The first evening of the crusade arrived and we had the PA equipment set up, the music planned and the lights on. We had even built benches for people to sit on. Everything was in place; we were ready for a great meeting.

I was keen to get out of my work clothes at last and to get up and preach. I said to Doris, "Honey, why don't you start playing your piano and sing a few choruses? Then when the people arrive and fill the place I'll begin ministering." It was 7.00pm and Doris began to play. She played and sang her heart out for the next thirty minutes – and not one person turned up! Not a soul had come to the meeting.

Every now and then we would hear the sound of a car and think, "Okay, here comes someone," but then they would pass by. The platform was just visible from the road and every now and then a bus full of people would slow down for a moment – perhaps out of curiosity – before moving away. Occasionally a car would almost stop, take a good look at the two of us stood by ourselves on the platform, honk their horn as if mocking us, then drive off!

After playing for half an hour Doris said, "I'm tired of playing and singing to no one!"

I said, "Okay, I'll go ahead and preach then."

"Preach?" she asked, amazed. "Who are you going to preach to?"

"Well," I replied, "we've worked for a whole month to prepare this place, I'm not leaving without preaching!"

"Okay," she said. "If that's what you want to do" and with that sat down to become my congregation of one.

I took my Bible, read a passage of Scripture, and began to preach to all those empty pews in front of me – just as though the place was full of people. You may wonder why! To me it was a statement of faith. I wasn't prepared to take no for an answer. I began preaching from the bottom of my heart, crying out to the open air that Jesus Christ saves, heals and delivers.

As I continued to preach, I looked up and saw a number of cows approaching. They were crossing the road onto our land and coming in via the new entrance to the property that we had created. These four Holstein cows kept on coming and didn't stop until they had walked all the way up the middle aisle, and all the way to the front of the platform. There they stopped and looked at me. I carried on preaching and the cows grazed on the grass, occasionally looking up at me and mooing. I preached my heart out to those cows. I was not going to be denied!

After another thirty minutes of ministering to cows I felt it was time to stop. We packed down our equipment and began to head back to the house we were renting for the duration of the crusade. Doris looked at me. "You do realize that you preached to four cows tonight?"

"Yes I do," I responded. "But those cows are going to give contented milk from this day forward!"

We both burst out laughing and continued to laugh all the way home. We were not discouraged. We figured that the most important thing was to be faithful to what God had called us to do, and to do it whether we had an audience or not. The next night twelve people turned up, so that was a 1200% improvement on the previous night!

We then continued with the crusade for the next seven months, until the lot was filled with people. After its inauspicious beginnings, it turned out to be a great work of God and we saw many souls saved, healed and delivered. We were given free time on television and much recognition through out the country. Today there is a great church in that city. It may have started with four cows, but now it is filled with hundreds of faithful believers! Never despise the small things. Stay faithful.

Don't be discouraged and continue doing what God has called you to do.

Available for service?

I once received a copy of the district newsletter from the State of Indiana, which was talking about upcoming events in the region that would be taking place that month and so forth. I was reading under the heading "News of Interest" when I came across the following advertisement. The person was offering their time and gifts in the service of the Lord … well, sort of… The heading in bold letters read, "AVAILABLE" and underneath it said, "I am open for full time service wherever the Lord may lead. I would be glad to accept evangelistic meetings – within a 35-40 mile radius of my hometown, Terre Haute".

I had to have a chuckle at this. What could this person be thinking? They were proclaiming that they were "available", to go "wherever the Lord may lead". But only, Lord, as long as you don't expect me to go more than, say, 35-40 miles from home – because that would be unreasonable, right? No offense, but I don't think this brother was ever going to be a world traveler.

I am not suggesting that you always need to go to foreign lands in order to be a missionary. You can be a missionary to the homeless people who lives on the streets of your hometown. You can be a missionary to your neighbors and community. The important thing is this: *you must be prepared to go wherever God leads.* And by "wherever" I mean "wherever"! God isn't looking for us to set parameters on our service to Him – He is just looking for our obedience.

Do you want to become a missionary?

"If you are allergic to dance, babies, beggars, chopped suet, cockroaches, curried crabs, duplicators, guitars, humidity and indifference, itches, jungles, mildew, minority groups, mud and poverty, sweat and unmarried mothers – you had better think twice before applying."

"Do you have the ability to mix with people, mix concrete, wade rivers, write articles, love one's neighbors, deliver babies, sit cross-legged on the floor, conduct meetings, drain swamps, digest questionable dishes, patch human weaknesses, suffer fools gladly and burn midnight oil? If you have the ability to do these few things, these are the qualifications for becoming a missionary in a foreign country. WELCOME."

I'll never forget the young lady who came to us on the mission field and told us that she was there to work with the children and that she wanted this to be her life's work. We were really excited for her and happy to have her in our camp. On her first evening with us, we wished her a good night's sleep and told her we'd see her in the morning. We had lots to do the next day.

In the morning, however, just as we were sitting down to plan the day's activities, this girl suddenly appeared with her suitcase all packed, ready to leave! When we asked what was going on she told us that, when she took her shower before bed, there were cockroaches three inches long in the shower. She said there was no was way she was staying under such conditions.

"I'm going home," she declared, "and don't look for me to come back!"

Seeing all the fuss, one of the locals asked me what had happened to her, since she was so animated and upset. I explained that she had lost her vision over *la cucaracha* (a cockroach). It wasn't funny at the time, but we laugh about it now.

Look out for the tall grass

In the June of 1969 Doris and I were attending a school of missions based in Springfield, Missouri. We would be studying full time and were looking forward to a wonderful time of learning and training, ready for the mission field. There were classes throughout the day and services in the evenings.

We arrived early on the first weekend. Classes began on Monday, so on Sunday night we wanted to find a local church to attend. We connected with a veteran missionary named Floyd Woodworth who told us he knew of a church just outside town that would be nice to attend, so we decided to make our way over there. It was dark as we pulled up the driveway of the parking lot alongside the church.

We commented to each other that it was surprising to see how tall the grass was in the parking lot. It was several feet tall. We got out of the car and began to walk, in the dark, towards the building. I went first,

Floyd behind me. After a minute or so, Floyd looked behind him and said, "Where's Doris?"

"Oh, she's just behind us," I said.

"No she's not," Floyd observed.

We both stopped and looked around. Doris was nowhere to be seen. We began looking around and calling for her until we heard a faint cry from somewhere near the car. It transpired that both me and Floyd, who was sitting directly behind me, had gotten out of the driver's side doors and begun to walk up the path. Doris, however, had gotten out of the other side and plunged straight down a deep ditch! The tall grass at the side of the drive had completely obscured the drop, so that she thought she was about to step on solid ground!

To our amazement, there she was, lying several feet down at the bottom of the ditch. I had missed driving into it by about a foot. She began to say that she thought she may have broken her leg, because she was in a lot of pain.

As you can imagine, it took a long time and a lot of effort for me and Floyd to get her out of the ditch, back into the car, and to the Emergency room of a local hospital. We were so upset that something like this could happen at church. You're supposed to go to church to get healed, not to get hurt!

Thankfully, Doris' leg was not broken, just severely sprained. But come Monday morning and the start of mission's school, there she was on a pair of crutches, feeling somewhat self-conscious. Plus our accommodation was on the second floor of the college, which had no elevator! Floyd and I would have to intertwine arms to make a "seat" to carry Doris up and down the stairs every time!

Hair raising flying adventure

Once Doris and I were flying out of Santa Marta to travel over the Andes Mountains to another city in Colombia called Bucaramanga. The airline, Avianca, had just purchased a "new plane", we were told. But when we were ready to board it, I noticed that it was a DC-3. There is no such thing as a new DC-3. They stopped making them years ago. By "new" they meant they had acquired a second-hand one, given it a fresh coat of paint and put their logo on it.

In due course, all the passengers were secure in their seats and we were ready to take off. The pilot taxied down the runway and lifted off, but at about 2,000ft the door of the plan flew open. The effect of this was so dramatic I thought that the entire back of the plane had fallen off. The wind and noise were horrendous! I turned to my right to see what had happened. I saw a Catholic priest, his face white as a sheet, furiously crossing himself and he feared for his life. If I had known one of those prayers I might have been doing the same thing! Instead I just called upon the Lord to keep His hand upon us and deploy His angels to protect us.

The plane quickly circled around and landed safely. The pilot came out to tell everyone to remain seated and assured us that everything was going to be just fine.

They would fix the door and shortly we would be on our way again. At this point I looked out of the window to see several men approaching the plane bearing sledgehammers and carrying ladders. Sure enough, the ladders were placed against the plane and a man with a sledgehammer began to beat and beat on the door. It sounded like someone pounding a fifty-five gallon steel drum! Eventually the hammering ceased and the men went away. Once again, the pilot assured us that all was well and we were ready to depart again.

We set off and, again, at around 2000ft, the door flew open for a second time! We were all frightened and the pilot looped back around and landed the plane again. Believe it or not, the same men came back with their ladders and sledgehammers. The pilot came out and said, "Just relax, we will fix the problem!"

In due course, after another round of incredibly loud hammering, we were told that all was well and we would attempt to depart for a third time. You would think that if we'd had any sense at all we would have exited that plane like lightning and been on our way, but no, we sat there and went along with it! Collectively we held our breath as we began to soar into the air again, waiting with morbid fascination to see if the door would fly open again. Thankfully, it didn't. Doris and I looked at each other, relieved.

"I guess they managed to fix it this time," Doris commented dryly.

We arrived in Bucaramanga a couple of hours later, relieved to be safely back on solid ground. But guess what? The door was so tightly hammered into place that they couldn't open it and we couldn't get out! We watched again as more men with ladders trooped out of the airport – taller ones this time because they needed to reach up to the cockpit window. They had to use crowbars to lever open the tiny windows. Then they passed a crowbar through to the pilot, who in turn came down the aisle and tried to pry open the door from the inside, while others applied force from outside.

We watched the mechanics at work – and I use the term "mechanics" lightly – until eventually the door popped open and we were all able to disembark. We did so laughing with the other passengers, who were all shaking hands and slapping each other on the back. We had all bonded quickly! We had arrived safe and sound and everything was going to be alright. For us, it was just another day on the mission field. We thanked God that He had gotten us where we needed to be safely, in the end!

* * *

All of this is funny in hindsight, of course, but it also has a serious side. We are called to persevere, despite the obstacles and difficulties we face – funny or otherwise.

Over the years we have encountered and endured many obstacles – cancer, kidney failure, and the threat of physical harm and danger in many countries. But God has always seen us through. He always remains faithful and we always emerge on the other side of trials and tribulations rejoicing and with a chuckle, saying, "Well it was interesting to see how God has brought us through another crisis." Praise God. He does have a sense of humor – and it *does* help if we have one too!

PART TWO

The Power Of Prayer

CHAPTER 9

The Importance of Prayer

Prayer for wisdom and discernment

*"Rejoice always, **pray without ceasing**,*
in everything give thanks;
for this is the will of God in Christ Jesus for you."
1 Thessalonians 5:16-18

Anyone who wants to serve God in any kind of full time ministry needs to learn how to become a prayer warrior. Prayer has been called the "central activity of a Christian". It is simply two-way communication between God and us. Without it, we cannot have a proper relationship with Him – just as a husband and wife couldn't have a proper relationship if they never, ever spoke to one another.

Both Doris and I are so grateful that we were raised by parents who took the issue of prayer seriously and persisted in prayer themselves. Prayer is as vital as breathing in and out is to our physical survival. Prayer is the oxygen of our spiritual lives.

Although the Bible tells us to make requests of God through prayer when we have particular needs, the truth is, the Lord constantly uses the process of prayer to speak into our hearts and to transform and shape us more into the image of His Son.

When we find ourselves thrust into situations we have never encountered before – which, on the mission field, are a frequent occurrence – prayer is the most powerful tool in our spiritual toolbox. There is a huge need for wisdom and discernment, especially when you are in the midst of an unfamiliar culture. In these situations God grows our faith through prayer.

Thankfully, the Bible tells us,

"But if any of you lacks wisdom, let him ask of God, who gives to all generously and without reproach, and it will be given to him." (James 1:5)

We have found this an essential part of ministry. We need the wisdom and guidance of God continually, and we access it through prayer, as the following story of how God orchestrated a little girl's miraculous healing illustrates.

We were holding a tent crusade In Cartago, Costa Rica. We were seeing many people saved and filled with the Holy Spirit. One evening, one of the families attending came to tell us of a young girl of seven who was in the children's hospital in the capital city, San Jose, asking whether we would pray for her.

This little girl had numerous tumors on her head – all over the top, across her forehead, at the base of her neck – and they were about the size of eggs. She had been hospitalized for a long time, but now she was so poorly that she was at the point of death. Her doctors said there was nothing more they could do for her because the roots of the tumors had spread into her brain. All she could do was to lie in her bed, where she cried out constantly, making a strange noise 24-hours a day.

Around the time we heard this little girl's story, the hospital had already sent her home to die. They felt she had but a few days at most. She hadn't eaten or drunk anything for several days and they knew there was no way a child could survive under such circumstances. The family lived in the neighboring town of El Tejar, close to Cartago, so I decided to visit their house and pray for this little girl. I had a young man called Hugo working alongside me who was going to be the pastor of the church we were planting, so I invited him to accompany me.

When we arrived at the house it seemed to be filled with a lot of people. I prayed and asked the Lord for wisdom and the Holy Spirit prompted me to clear everyone out of the house, and especially out of the bedroom where the little girl was, apart from her parents.

We entered the bedroom and there was this poor child, crying out with this weird noise. We approached her bed and then the Holy Spirit spoke to me and told me that we should not lay hands on her, or touch her to anoint her with oil. I didn't exactly know why, but I just obeyed. I later found out that the town of El Tejar was notorious for its witchcraft and it's possible that the parents might have thought that we were using some kind of "magic potion" to restore the child's health.

Pastor Hugo and I knelt down on the bedroom floor and prayed. After a time of intense prayer we both looked up, confident that the Lord had touched her. We both sensed it in our spirits. We got up from the floor and I turned to her parents and told them emphatically, "Your daughter is healed." They looked over my shoulder at their daughter, who was still lying in her bed making this hideous noise, and then looked back at me in disbelief. But I knew that I knew that God had intervened and heard our prayers. Both Hugo and I felt an immense peace in our hearts. God had healed her, even if the evidence wasn't immediately available.

We left the house to get back to the town of Cartago and continue our tent crusade. By the time we returned it was time to start the evening service. We had a great time and, in due course, packed down our equipment and returned home to rest. The next day there seemed to be a commotion taking place in the town. People were talking and there seemed to be some something happening, but we didn't find out what. The day passed and then it was time for the next evening meeting.

That night I stood on the platform and spotted the parents of the little girl we'd prayed for. They were making their way to the front of the meeting and approaching the platform, bringing the girl's grandmother and other extended family members with them. They began to climb up onto the platform and it wasn't until the last second that I noticed the little girl was with them too. This is the testimony they gave to everyone assembled there:

"Early this morning, while my husband and I were still asleep in bed, our daughter came into the room and shook me, saying, 'Mommy, I'm hungry. I want to eat.' She had not eaten or drunk anything for four days. So we jumped out of bed and gave her food and water. She began to eat a little and drink some water and then began to talk to us as if nothing had ever happened."

Every one of the large tumors protruding from her head had vanished. She had been miraculously healed by the power of God. Her had rejoiced and shouted, "She is healed, she is healed!"

The story of this outstanding healing spread fast through the little town where they were living and many people flocked to our crusade meetings as a result. The revival continued and we were privileged to see many more manifestations of the power of God.

Prayer works!

CHAPTER 10

Prayer – Doorway To The Miraculous
(by Doris Burns)

Prayer for healing

"Now faith is the assurance of things hoped for, the conviction of things not seen."
(Hebrews 11:1 NASB)

The writer of Hebrews reminds us that when we pray, we pray in faith. And faith is the confident assurance that God will hear our prayers and answer. It is the assurance that something is going to happen. The certainty that what we hope for is waiting for us ahead – even though at present we cannot see it.

Some may ask, "Why does God need us to pray when He already knows what we need?" But it is through prayer, and dependency on the Lord, that we grow in faith and are filled with hope.

In chapters six and seven we recounted the story of the great revival mission in Cartagena, Colombia. During that crusade we witnessed many miracles. But parallel to this we faced a serious challenge and threat as I became very ill. I want to share the testimony of what happened and show how God answers our prayers in times of need.

We were all very excited to be in Cartagena to plant some new churches, but we had only been there about three months when I became sick. I went to see a local doctor and he prescribed antibiotics for what he thought was a tropical infection. I took the medication, but in spite of it my condition continued to worsen.

Eventually I had to be admitted to the local hospital. The surgeon in charge was a very fine man and a specialist in his particular field, but none of the hospitals in the city were well equipped or had sufficient supplies of medicines. In fact, the nurses – some of whom were working there having had only two weeks of training – were constantly going out to the local pharmacy to buy medication and bring it back to the hospital.

The surgeon carried out some exploratory surgery on me and the prognosis was not good. He suspected the cause of the illness was cancer-related and said it was beyond the capacity of the hospital's facilities to treat me. He didn't know what else he could do for me.

Franklin stayed with me constantly. I was in hospital for five days before I was released to go home with just some antibiotics. I was very sick and had an extremely low blood count. The phone system in Cartagena left much to be desired and Franklin spend three days trying to call my parents to let them know what was happening.

I continued to deteriorate over those days and eventually the local doctor told Franklin that he must get me back to the US where I could be treated properly. But first we had to get permission from our mission board to come home. We finally got that approval and then we had to get the paperwork done in order to leave Colombia. This process usually took two weeks! Thank God He was in control and within twenty-four hours we were cleared to leave.

We flew to New Orleans, Louisiana. A specialist there was waiting to see me when we arrived at West Jefferson Hospital. After reading all the paperwork and records he scheduled me for surgery the next morning, July 12, 1972. He told us that he didn't know what else to do – he had to physically investigate what was wrong with me. We agreed that this was the right thing to do, but we prayed earnestly and asked God to intervene. We believed God and trusted Him to do some kind of miracle.

After another operation I was in hospital a further seven days until I was released to go and recover at Franklin's brother's home in Buras, Louisiana. Lots of my family was there and my parents had traveled from Oklahoma. I still didn't get any better, however. In fact, each day I got worse until, one day, the incision I'd had burst open and I began seriously hemorrhaging. I was rushed back to hospital in New Orleans at around four in the morning. By the time I was admitted I had lost a tremendous amount of blood.

The surgeon decided to operate immediately. He actually came out and told Franklin and the girls to say goodbye to me, because I was unlikely to make it.

The girls were just nine and ten years old at this point, but they knew how to pray. Along with some other family members who had come along, they knelt down around me in the emergency room and began to cry out to God.

Everyone was praying in English and then I heard something really strange. I realized that my sister-in-law, Betty, was praying beautifully in fluent Spanish. What was strange about this was that Betty didn't speak a word of Spanish! I knew that the prayer must be coming directly from Heaven: *"Te llamo, te llamo y no voy a dejarte."*

I prayed and said, "Lord, let me hear that one more time." Again Betty spoke in fluent Spanish, *"Te llamo, te llamo y yo no voy a dejarte."* In English it means, "I have called you, I have called you and I will not leave you." I thanked God for His Holy Spirit and a great peace washed over me.

They took me out to surgery for the third time, but I had perfect peace because I knew my Jesus was in control. Afterwards, my stomach was wrapped in octopus bandages with clamps to hold my incision together. The surgeon came into the recovery room and was surprised to see me still alive. I remained in hospital for another week before being released once again to go back to Buras with the family. My parents needed to return to Oklahoma, so they took the girls to look after them for us.

Once again, the prognosis of the doctors was that I was not going to live, so they advised Franklin to arrange to take me wherever I wanted to go. He arranged for flights to Lawton, Oklahoma where my dad met us with an ambulance to take me on to their home in Snyder, Oklahoma. I still had peace in my heart!

The problems continued, so I was sent to a doctor in Lawton, Oklahoma. I took all of my records. He read them and then examined me and said that my intestines and colon were filled with cancerous tumors and I needed another operation. He said he believed I had a 50-50 chance. The surgery was scheduled it for November 25th. I went back home and continued to pray and the Lord gave me a scripture:

"Jesus said to her, 'Did I not say to you that if you believe, you will see the glory of God?'" (John 11:40)

Peace flooded my heart again!

Franklin was called to Miami, Oklahoma to preach at Sunday morning and evening missions services. The girls and I stayed home. He called that night and said revival had broken out and there were lots of miracles. Pastor Baser wanted him to preach a few more nights. His older brother was with him. I assured him I would be okay. The next weekend, my sister-in-law Betty, called to ask if I would like to go up for the weekend services. I was very weak, but said yes. She made a bed in the back seat of her car, put me in and drove the 300 miles to the meeting. I was scheduled for surgery the next week.

I was sitting in the service and a group of ladies all gathered around to pray for me. They had been fasting and praying for my healing and were sure that God was going to heal me that night. The Lord spoke to me while they were praying and said, "Go home, call your doctor and cancel your surgery." I felt so weak I could hardly stand, but nevertheless I stood up and announced what God had said to me.

The next morning I called my doctor to tell him I was canceling my surgery. He informed me that I was crazy and I was going to die. He was a confirmed atheist, so he didn't believe in God and had no time for my faith. I insisted, however, and that was that.

Two weeks went by and I was worse than before. Our friends kept saying I should go to the hospital. Franklin was still at the revival in Miami, Oklahoma. My mother finally called him on the Friday night to let him know the situation. He left after the Friday night service and drove all night to get home. On the Saturday morning, however, Franklin told me that he felt God had not finished with him in Miami. I simply told him, "Make me a bed in the back seat of the car, go back, and take me with you." So he did.

On Sunday night, when Franklin got up to preach, he announced that God had told him to stop fasting because He had answered his prayer. Then the Lord spoke to me and said, "Stand up and tell this congregation that you are healed." I did. That was December 3, 1972. The next day we returned home to Snyder. I had one more week of severe sickness and pain. But on Friday morning, December 10, I woke up and all the pain was gone. I was healed. I called the doctor and told him I needed to see him immediately. When I arrived at his office I told him to go ahead and do all the testing and blood work he needed to, because I was healed.

After he had finished with his testing, the same atheist doctor walked out with his hands in the air. "I cannot find anything wrong," he told me. "Everything is healed. You need no medication and you can go wherever you want to. I don't need to see you again." He gladly wrote a letter to our foreign missions board to let them know I had a medical clearance.

By the January of 1973 we were back in Cartagena, Colombia, and preaching at the crusade in the stadium. I played my accordion and sang every night. We saw a huge number of awesome miracles.

I have been blessed to minister and share this testimony around the world. I pray for people and see many miracles. People often ask me to *explain* what happened. But I can't. All I can say is that Jesus endured the stripes on His back for our healing and through the power of prayer, we can be healed. I am just a messenger. He is the Healer.

There is no understanding a miracle

I learned a long time ago not to keep asking God "Why?" We have to learn to live beyond the whys. Perhaps that is why I so strongly believed His promise for my healing. Here is a second testimony of how God delivered me from serious sickness.

In March 1976 my husband Franklin and I were conducting a Good News Crusade in Surinam, South America. We were seeing tremendous miracles of healing and people who were being delivered from demonic possession.

One night I became very ill. I had severe pain in my chest and back and I couldn't keep anything in my stomach. After a few days my legs began to swell and my kidneys were not functioning properly. We decided we needed to return to Lawton, Oklahoma, to see the doctor who had taken care of me when I had cancer.

Political problems in Surinam meant that we had to sit on the plane in Georgetown, Guyana, for five hours in the blazing heat before we managed to make it home. The doctor immediately ruled out any connection with my previous illness. "Everything in there is in perfect condition," he told me. But he suggested we should have x-rays made of my kidneys. I was admitted and tests were made, including an arteriogram – a test of the artery leading to the kidneys.

When the results came in, my doctor explained them to me. He said the test showed my left kidney was completely dead and the right kidney was not functioning properly. Also there were spots on the kidneys that the doctors could not identify. He suggested an operation to remove the left kidney, but due to the infection in my body, the surgery was postponed while I was given antibiotics.

At this point I couldn't travel any more, so we relocated to Dennison, Texas. There we met a friend who was on a dialysis machine because of a kidney malfunction. He told me, "Doris, don't let the doctor remove your kidney without further consultation from another doctor." He suggested that I visit the Mayo Clinic in Rochester, Minnesota, where he was a regular patient and I agreed. On June 8, three months since I had become ill, I visited the clinic. They studied the test made in Oklahoma and started me on several types of exercise to assist the function of my kidneys. After 10 days I went in to see the specialist at the clinic. He said, "You have some very serious problems. Your left kidney doesn't function at all and your right kidney only functions about 25 percent of the time." He too recommended the removal of my left kidney and scheduled the operation for two weeks later, on July 12.

I went home and the Lord gave me a dream. In the dream He told me that the surgeon would be able to repair my left kidney and that I would experience very little pain. A couple of days later some of our relatives asked me if I feared the surgery, so I told them about my dream. At that point Franklin spoke up. He had had the same dream on the same night!

I entered the Mayo clinic hospital on July 11. The next day I was in surgery for eight hours and then in recovery for several more hours. When I woke up Franklin was beside my bed and he whispered in my ear, "You did not lose your kidney!" The surgeon had been able to repair it. In fact, he commented that it was the most successful kidney operation he had ever done.

After surgery I was in the hospital for fourteen days with about seven tubes running out of my side. In all that time I only had two pain shots. I was allowed to return home, but scheduled to be back in January 1977. The doctor said he would x-ray the left kidney at that time and make sure it was functioning properly. If so, he would operate on the right kidney, which had enlarged to twice its normal size, and attempt to repair it. He told me there was no possible way I could ever go back to South America. He wrote a letter to our mission's board explaining this, so we had to make a decision.

A few months later we were called to pastor First Assembly of God church in Athens, Texas. We witnessed many miracles there and were happy to see the church grow in number. We also established a strong missions program. The congregation, and especially the ladies of the church, prayed earnestly for my complete healing. They knew our hearts were on the mission field. In January 1977 we went back to Rochester, Minnesota. The x-rays that had previously taken three hours to process were ready in about ten minutes, so I knew something must have happened. The doctor called us in to look at the x-rays. He was shaking his head in disbelief and saying, "You know, this is good!"

After a detailed explanation of the x-rays he said, "I notice on your records that you are missionaries to South America and that you could not go back because you didn't have medical clearance?" We told him that was correct. Then he said, "Well, you are on your way back to South America. Both kidneys are functioning 100 percent and you don't need any more surgery." In June 1977 we returned to the mission field.

When we left the clinic that day in January, the doctor told me he would not need to see me any more and that I needed no medication. I still don't take medication to this day, nor am I on any special diet, and am in perfect health.

Thank God for people who believe His Word and are prepared to persist in prayer!

CHAPTER 11

There Is Nothing Too Hard For The Lord

Praying in faith

"And whatever you ask in prayer, you will receive, if you have faith."
(Matthew 21:22)

I will never forget the excitement that was in our hearts as we moved into the city of Guadalajara, Mexico. It has a population of several million people and a beautiful, subtropical climate. We loved the people and the food and culture of the city and it has become a place very dear to our hearts.

We knew that we would be living here for at least a few months. In fact, those few months turned into three years before we were finished there. Our initial plan had been to put up one tent and hold one crusade in order to raise up a church there. But our missions board asked me to become the evangelism coordinator for that area, and so we were able to put up five tents in different locations across this great city and run five crusades.

Some other evangelist friends helped us in this, sharing the preaching duties so that we could run extended crusades for several months across the locations. We were able to build five churches practically simultaneously because other teams of men and youths came from the US to help us. What a blessing!

I began the first crusade in the first tent. We formed an evangelistic team, added musicians and singers, and had an awesome time. We were privileged to witness many people coming to know Jesus Christ as their Lord and Savior with many miracles.

On one particular Sunday night I asked everyone who needed a miracle in their life to come forward and form a line to receive prayer. Our staff was busy organizing the people so that every single person could be prayed for and attended to. I was just finishing preaching a message entitled, "With God, nothing shall be impossible".

Turning to begin ministering to the assembled people, I was confronted with a lady who had come forward for prayer with her husband at her side. She introduced herself as Elena.

"You said that with God nothing is impossible," she began. I was feeling confident and full of faith at that moment, so I responded,

"Yes ma'am, that is the absolute truth – with God nothing is impossible!"

She was wearing a long dress that reached the floor. Without another word she reached down and pulled the dress up above her knees and asked me to look at her legs. It was a shocking sight. Her legs looked so pathetic I didn't know how she was even able to stand. There was hardly any flesh on her legs and on her shins the skin was so thin that part of the bone was exposed.

"I'm diabetic," she explained, "and my doctor is afraid that gangrene has set in. I am due to check into the hospital tomorrow, on Monday, so that they can operate on me on Tuesday. They are going to amputate both of my legs from above the knees."

I looked at the shocking state of this lady's legs and all I could hear were my own words, going round and around my head: *I just told this lady that nothing was impossible … now what am I going to do?!*

The Holy Spirit graciously spoke into my heart and I realized, once again, that there was nothing that I could personally do to heal her. I could only do what the Lord had commanded – to *"lay hands on the sick and they shall recover"* (Mark 16:18). I told her were going to pray, lay hands on her, and ask God to do a miracle for her.

We did just that. As we prayed, I sensed the anointing of the Holy Spirit in a special way. I kept thinking how she must feel, knowing that she had to go into the hospital and in two day's time she would lose both her legs. Sometimes we feel so small and weak in the face of the immense need of others. At the same time, we realize that we are just the messengers of Almighty God and it is He who can transform people's circumstances. We are simply pointing people to the One who received the stripes upon His back for our healing – the Lord Jesus.

As we prayed I declared to Elena, "In the name of Jesus, the Lord and Savior, you are healed. Legs, I command you to be healed in the name of Jesus."

After prayer, with the help of her husband, she walked out of the tent through one of the side curtains and got into a vehicle. I watched them drive away. For the rest of that night I kept thinking about her.

"Lord, we have prayed," I said. "We have believed and we have thanked you in advance for the miracle. I am not asking you to do it again – I just want to give thanks to you for what you have already done."

The next evening the crusade continued. Just before it began, I noticed a large truck pull up alongside the tent. Some twenty-five to thirty people climbed out of it. Then a van pulled up behind it and several more people got out. Finally, a car arrived and I spotted Elena getting out of the car with some friends. This large group proceeded to fill up one side of the tent.

The service started, the musicians played and the singers sang. I could feel a special anointing of the Lord as I got up to preach. All the time, however, my eyes were fixed on Elena.

"She told me she was checking into the hospital," I thought to myself, "but here she is, and surrounded by all these people. Something has happened!"

There was clearly a buzz of excitement running through this group and lots of whispering. I made an attempt to carry on with my message and read some scriptures, but eventually I had to give up and say something. I addressed Elena directly.

"Ma'am, are you wanting to say something?"

Immediately she jumped to her feet and asked if she could come onto the platform. "Please do," I responded. "Come right up here." She came and stood next to me on the stage, then turned to face the congregation and told everyone that she had a testimony to share.

"I want to tell everyone what happened to me at four o' clock this morning. I was half asleep and thinking about the fact that this morning I was due to go into hospital. But then I began to feel my legs tingling. It was a sensation unlike anything I'd ever felt before. It was so strong that I sat up to look at my legs and I could not believe what I was seeing. I grabbed my husband and said, 'Look! Look at my legs!' He was half asleep too and he murmured, 'Honey, I've seen your legs.' But I said, 'Yes, but you've never seen them like this!'

At this point, full of excitement and with no modesty whatsoever, Elena hitched up her dress to about mid thigh and showed her legs to everyone. In actual fact, I don't think there was any place for modesty right then. She was bouncing up and down and saying, "Look at my legs!"

We all looked. All of the flesh on her legs had been restored. The bones were not exposed. There was none of the lacerations or marks that I had seen there previously. Her legs looked brand new, with skin as flawless as that of a newborn child. She had been miraculously and wonderfully healed. Together we all shouted and praised God!

Later that week Elena got her doctor to confirm the healing and to take photographs and x-rays of her legs, so that she had concrete evidence she could show to others. From then on, everywhere she went she told people about how God had healed her. Her great testimony, proclaiming the healing power of the Lord Jesus, was instrumental in opening the door for us to begin a second crusade several months later. As more crusades were begun, we continued to see God do miracles and churches were birthed.

These were glorious times in this city. To this day, whenever we go back there to visit, if we are in a hotel or restaurant, there are still people who approach us to recall the wonderful things they saw during the tent crusades.

Let me encourage you. Whatever challenges you may be facing in your life right now, there is nothing impossible with God! You too can proclaim His mercy, His goodness, His grace and His power. For, *"Jesus Christ is the same yesterday and today and forever"* (Hebrews 13:8).

CHAPTER 12

From The Mouths of Babes

Prayers of childlike faith

Once we traveled to West Texas to conduct revival meetings at a particular city. During one meeting the pastor became rapidly sick and looked deathly ill. He immediately took to his bed and the next day Doris and I went to visit him to pray for him.

He was a very large man of some 360 pounds, and as Doris and I entered his bedroom in the basement of his parsonage, we saw this mountain of a man lying on his bed, clearly very sick. Just as we were about to begin praying, however, his small five-year-old son, David, came running into the room and stood by his dad.

"Do you want me to pray for you daddy?" he asked earnestly.

His father rolled over with some effort and saw the sincerity in his son's eyes.

"Sure son," he said, "pray for me. That would be nice."

We stood back to let the boy pray. Little David, with a serious look on his face, laid his hands right in the middle of his dad's stomach and prayed the following prayer of faith:

"Thank you Lord for this food! Amen!"

With that, he took off running. We all stood there looking at one another for a moment and then burst out laughing. But then, to our amazement, the pastor sat straight up in bed and declared, "I felt a touch of God. I'm healed!"

We left the room so that the pastor could get dressed and presently he came upstairs and had something to eat with the rest of the family. That night he was at the revival meeting, completely well.

The words we use in prayer are not nearly as important as our faith and expectancy!

Childlike faith

God often uses children to teach us lessons in "childlike" faith. On the mission field in Latin America we had a large Airedale dog named Sparty. We all loved him very much. More than a pet, he was a faithful companion and the protector of our children. When I say he was their *protector*, I mean that we could not even discipline our girls if Sparty was around, he was so protective of them.

On one occasion we were all rolling around on the living room floor, wrestling and having a good old time tickling and rough-housing with our girls. They were laughing and squealing and just having a blast. All of a sudden we heard a loud noise as Sparty, who had been outside, came bursting through the back door and raced down the corridor to the lounge to come to their aid.

This in itself was somewhat comical, because we had cement floors in that house and as Sparty attempted to round the corner to rescue the girls, he struggled to gain traction on the slippery floor and was sliding all over the place. However, I noticed that his lips were curled and his teeth bared and I knew, "This dog is serious! He things I'm hurting these girls!" He didn't understand we were just playing a game.

We immediately stopped and called to him, "Hey Sparty, come here boy. Everything's okay!" He calmed down and began wagging his tail, reassured. I learned two things that day: one, that Sparty was a great protector of our kids, and two, that I couldn't discipline them while he was present. He made a believer out of me!

One day, some two years later, Sharon my youngest daughter came to tell me that Sparty was sick. I went to check on him and there he was lying on the patio, looking sick and lifeless, with greenish foam coming out of his mouth. I called the vet to come to the house and examine him.

In due course, the vet arrived and examined the dog. He told me that Sparty had hepatitis and was very sick. In fact, he struggled to detect much of a heartbeat and said he believed the dog would be dead in a matter of a few hours. The vet suggested I let him take Sparty away with him to his clinic where he would see what, if anything, he could do – it wouldn't be good just to let him die there at the house, in front of the girls.

I agreed and gave him permission to take Sparty away. A couple of hours later the vet called me to say that the dog was at the point of death and that I should give him permission to give him a shot and put him down. There was no point in prolonging his suffering, because his condition was terminal. I told the vet that Sparty had been a great, loyal friend to us for many years and that I certainly didn't want him to suffer unnecessarily if he was going to die anyway. The vet said he would take care of it right away.

Of course, I was now faced with the unpleasant task of letting our girls know that Sparty had gone away and wasn't coming back; that sadly he was sick and had died. I did my best to convey this to them. Then Sharon, who was nine years old at the time, piped up:

"No daddy, I've been praying for Sparty and he is coming back!"

You can imagine how I felt at that moment. I had already given the vet permission to give Sparty the shot and he had confirmed he would do it right away. As far as I knew, the dog was already dead. I tried again to explain that Sparty was dead, so there was no way he was coming back, but once again Sharon assured me that he was healed.

"Daddy, I have prayed for Sparty and he will be back," she insisted.

"Okay honey," I said, "that's fine, that's good..."

I tried to console her as best as I could, then I had to leave to check on the progress of the mission we were currently involved in.

I returned home later that afternoon and to my amazement, I was greeted at the front door by Sparty – jumping up and down, running round and round in circles as though nothing had happened. I could not believe my eyes. "How in the world has this dog come back to us?" I wondered. "The vet told me he was giving him a shot and here he is, alive and well!"

Doris told me that after I had gone out the vet had called. He said that he had prepared the fatal shot for Sparty and, just as he was able to stick the needle in, Sparty had suddenly jumped up and leapt off the table! In fact, he was so "full of life" that it had taken the vet quite some time to corral him and place a muzzle on him. Returning him to our house, the astonished vet told Doris,

"This dog is more full of life than any dog I've ever seen! Take him. He's fine!"

I played with Sparty for a while, happy to see him again, and patted him on the head. I looked at Sharon, who just said to me,

"Daddy, I told you he was coming back, that he was healed!"

"Yes ma'am," I replied, "you were right and I was wrong!"

I think it's amazing that God is so kind that He is mindful of all our needs. He knew that Sparty was such a great companion to us all that He heard a little girl's prayers and healed our dog. What an awesome and caring God we serve.

It also taught me a great lesson about how our Heavenly Father responds to childlike simplicity in faith. As adults, we often turn faith into something complicated. In fact, it's very simple – our God knows and understands our needs, and He is delighted when we pray to Him and ask in faith.

CHAPTER 13

Don't Blow It!

Perseverance, patience and persistence in prayer

*"Be joyful in hope, patient in
affliction, faithful in prayer."*
(Romans 12:12)

Whenever our family was back in the US for a while, I always enjoyed visiting the health club and gym in my hometown. It's not a large town, so it was always pretty easy to get acquainted with everyone who attended the gym and it was good to spend time there. I worked out and stayed as fit as I could because it was always hard work putting up large tents, slinging a sledgehammer to drive in the stakes, then building the platform. I thought it wise to stay in shape so that I could continue to meet the physical demands of the task.

The owner of my local club was a Mr. Johnson. He was a well-built guy, in his mid-thirties, and fit, as one might expect. He was a nice guy and a friend, but for reasons best known to himself, he thought it funny to publicly single me out every time I turned up at the club.

"Hey preacher!" he would yell loudly in front of everyone. "What are you doing here? What are you preachers doing working out all the time?"

Everyone knew everyone in this small town, so my other friends and acquaintances would just raise their eyebrows or mutter, "What's his problem?"

Although I found it very annoying, I thought it best to just let him have his fun. I'd suffered worse verbal abuse in my time, so I just let him call me out and make his remarks. I figured he would get tired of it and stop in due course. To my surprise, he never let up! Every single time I went to the gym I was greeted with a loud, "Hey preacher!" followed by some other sarcastic remark.

On a number of occasions, my irritation rose up and I was ready to confront him. I wanted to say, "Man, just what is your problem? Why don't you shut up and leave me alone?" Thankfully, I didn't say these words, much as I wished I could. I just wanted to know why this "friend" insisted on ridiculing me in front of everyone at the club. I didn't understand what it was all about and wanted to put him in his place. Each time I felt that way and the words were on the tip of my tongue, however, the Holy Spirit checked me and I knew I had to bite my tongue and leave him be.

In due course we were preparing to leave the country again for Latin America, and from there to journey onwards to Central America. Our initial plan was to be gone for four months, then we would see what God had prepared for us to do and discover whether He wanted us to remain longer.

There was time for one more trip to the health club before we departed. I was standing by one of the weight machines when I noticed Mr. Johnson come in. "Here we go," I thought. "Prepare yourself for one more onslaught!" To my surprise, he didn't say a word, but approached me, somewhat gingerly, in complete silence. "What is he up to now?" I wondered.

I was amazed when he came up to me, threw his arms around me, and began to hug me. Was this another elaborate set up for him to poke fun at me? I was concerned about what everyone else at the gym thought about his strange behavior, and was looking around to see their reaction. Then all of a sudden he laid his head on my shoulder and began to say, "Please pray for me, please pray for me. I have just found out that I have cancer. It's already spread through my body and I need prayer. Will you please pray for me?"

You can imagine how I felt at that moment. I recalled how many times I had just wanted to tell him to shut up and leave me alone. I was profoundly grateful that the Lord had held me back each time. Now, because I had never so much as murmured a complaint in response to his baiting, here he was asking for prayer. I put my arms around him and prayed for him as I held him, pouring out my heart to God, right there in the gym. He thanked me over and over before he left.

We left for our missions trip and returned home after several months. As was my custom, I headed down to the health club to work out. As soon as I arrived, a number of different friends asked if I'd heard what had happened to Mr. Johnson while I'd been away. I hadn't.

In those days, before the prevalence of the Internet, we rarely got news from home.

They told me about his rapid and shocking deterioration. Everyone could see that he was obviously very ill and his doctor confirmed the rapid and widespread onset of cancer. This fit, healthy, 200lb man dropped to a little over 100lb in no time at all and then after a time, no one saw him any more.

Shortly after this, I received a phone call from the local doctor, Dr. Lemmon – a friend and also doctor to Mr. Johnson. He said he had a message to pass on to me. I couldn't imagine what it was. He told me that Mr. Johnson had died and he was with him when it happened. He said,

"As I stood at his bedside and he was taking his last few breaths, he gripped my hand and said, 'I want you to tell Franklin that everything is okay. I see Jesus standing at the foot of my bed. Everything is all right now. Tell him everything's okay.' He continued to tell me he could see Jesus standing next to him and then peacefully drifted away."

Peace flooded my being and I told Dr. Lemmon what an awesome thing this was, thanking him for passing on the message.

"I knew that I had to call you," Dr. Lemmon told me. "I knew that I had to honor his last request and I thought you would understand."

I thanked him again and hung up. I was so grateful to God that I didn't blow it and lose my temper with Mr.

Johnson. As a result he was ushered into eternity with the Lord Jesus.

We are called to persevere with patience and to continue to do good to others. Often we don't see the reason why, unless God in His grace reveals it to us. But whether He does or He doesn't, we keep on praying and we keep on persevering.

PART THREE

With Vision Comes Provision

CHAPTER 14

Where There is Vision, There is Always Provision

Over all our years in ministry, it has been amazing to see how God has always provided for our needs. There are so many stories to tell, we just had to have a section of the book dedicated to giving glory to God for His care and provision.

The writer of Hebrews prays the prayer, *"Now may the God of peace ... the great Shepherd of the sheep ... equip you with all you need for doing His will"* (Hebrews 13:20-21 NLT). And in Psalm 37:5 we are urged to, *"Depend on the Lord; trust Him and He will take care of you."* God is committed to caring for us – especially when we are set on doing His will. There are Bible verses too numerous to list here confirming His commitment to His children, but suffice to say, we know the truth of the verse,

"And my God will supply every need of yours according to his riches in glory in Christ Jesus." (Philippians 4:19 ESV)

God never gives someone a vision without following it up with provision. Every time God has spoken to us to go to a new country to establish a church and build His Kingdom, He has provided all we have needed.

It has not always been about material things – though He has provided those – but also about people. Teams of people from various different ministries have been willing to help fulfill the vision that God has put in our hearts and have given of their time and talents to serve the Lord alongside us.

Yes, there have been cars, trucks, motor homes, fifth wheel trailers, boats, motorcycles, saddles, PA equipment and money we needed to carry out the vision God gave us. God has never failed to provide what we needed to carry out whatever task He set before us. But key to fulfilling God's plans are willing servants. Over the years we have been hugely blessed by various people who helped us tremendously, expecting nothing in return. They were willing to give of themselves, their finances, and their gifting to help establish the Church of our Lord Jesus on foreign soil. We thank God for all of them!

Some time ago I was invited to a convention that was being conducted at a Bible School. The keynote speaker was an officer in the military, who had just returned home after serving in Afghanistan and Iraq. As a former military serviceman myself in years past, his inspiring message really connected with me, and I fully understood all he had to share about the way in which the military worked. I had experienced it myself as a serviceman, and I had experienced it on many continents planting churches.

He spoke about the great misconception the general public has about the military that most soldiers are fighting on the frontline of wars. In actual fact, only around 5% of all the soldiers based in Afghanistan and Iraq were engaged in frontline combat. 95% of the personnel were behind the lines performing the numerous tasks necessary to support the frontline troops, so that they were able to fulfill their mission.

Many of the supporting soldiers worked, for instance, in the Motor Pool. Transportation is a vital part of any military campaign as equipment is moved back and forth. There are medical teams working to ensure that the troops are in top condition. Office personnel endeavor to ensure that everything is highly organized, in the right place at the right time. The catering department is constantly cooking in shifts. Quartermasters control the supply of ammunition, arms and other equipment. The list goes on. The reality is, the majority do the diligent work that ensures the few are successful in combat on the frontline.

This is so like the work needed on foreign mission fields. It takes an army of people from all walks of life, with many gifts and talents, working together so that others are capable of carrying out their mission. Teams of people give up their vacation time and use their own finances to spend days, sometimes weeks, helping us to construct new church buildings. Young people come to help carry our door-to-door evangelism, handing out literature and inviting people to the crusade. Groups of people club together to raise money to buy us vehicles. Ladies raise money to buy furnishings for our new house in the mission location. Men raise money through ministries such as *Light For The Lost* to provide all the

Bibles and literature needed for the people who get saved. Pastors come and help mix concrete, lay bricks, and put down floors.

Then there are those who came to help minister in our crusades. Doris and I have been blessed to have many godly men, women and young boys and girls, who came to pray, counsel and preach.

Whenever a missionary stands in a pulpit to speak about all the things he or she is doing, you can be sure it has not been done alone. Nothing could be further from the truth. Behind every work of God is an army of believers who give of themselves sacrificially for the cause of the Kingdom. Thank the Lord for the willingness of so many to work "behind the lines" and bring us the equipment and necessities to get the job done.

There are so many people we could mention who have given of themselves to assist the work of the Lord. I will mention just a couple, whilst reiterating our appreciation for every single person who has helped in any way.

There were people who were missionaries in their own right who helped us, like Mike Hines, who came all the way to Colombia in his small airplane and airdropped literature from the sky. He flew his plane over many of the remote towns and villages of the Andes Mountains in order to distribute 20,000 cards for the "International Correspondence Institute". We had around 5,000 people respond, enrolling into the program.

Then there was Randy Parker, who passed away on March 31, 2014, and his wife Sarah. We are profoundly grateful for their support for over thirty-two years. Words can hardly express what a blessing they have both been to our family.

In chapter ten we recounted the story of Doris' kidney failure and subsequent healing. During that period we were invited to dinner by some friends from Athens, Texas. It was here that Randy came and introduced himself to us, saying that he had heard good things about our missionary work. He placed $100 bill in my hand. I cannot adequately express what a blessing and encouragement that was at such a testing time. Since then Randy and Sarah have frequently blessed us with years of prayer, love, friendship and finance.

One Christmas in the 1980s we were at Randy and Sarah's home for dinner. We had various projects that needed finance, but also some personal needs for our girls and ourselves. Quietly, Randy slipped a check into my pocket without a word. When we returned to the place where we were staying, I took out the check and handed it to Doris. We looked at it and began to praise God for His provision and Randy's generosity, that he had given us a check for $500. We were rejoicing with our girls when we stopped and looked again at the check, realizing that it was actually a check for $5,000! Then we all cried and praised God.

In 1987 this wonderful couple bought us a home in Athens, Texas, building us a beautiful home at 203 Crestview and helping us to arrange financing. A few months after this they gave us the money needed to relocate my mother from Louisiana to a nursing home in Chandler. In 1993 we came home from Saltillo needing a home. Once again Randy and Sarah gave us $20,000 for a down payment on 216 Crestview.

Many, many times, besides monthly support, they gave us special offerings to plant churches. In Christmas 2001 they let us move into a ranch house they owned and gave us a place to call home for an entire year.

Our dear friends' support has continued faithfully for thirty-two years. We wanted to use these pages to say "thank you" in some small way, for all the sacrificial love, support and encouragement. Thousands of souls around the world have been brought into the Kingdom because of Randy and Sarah. Lives have been changed forever.

Thanks be to God for His amazing, outstanding provision through people!

CHAPTER 15

Possum Kingdom and Beyond

I believe that everyone needs a Possum Kingdom in their life – and especially in their ministry – if they are going to do exploits for the Kingdom of God. "Possum Kingdom" is the place where our faith, and belief in God's commitment to provide for us, is tested and refined.

It was January 1961 when I arrived home having finished my military service and in the February I met with our denomination's credentialing committee to get my license to preach. On March 10, Doris and I were married in the little town of Moody, Texas, by our dear friend and superintendent, Rev. E. R. Anderson. By April we had moved to the small town of Graford, near Possum Kingdom, Texas. We were told that it would be a good place for us to launch our ministry.

So, married for just one month, we moved to a new town to take on a church that had been shut down for nearly two years. There was no pastor and no people. All that was left was an empty church building and a parsonage.

One of the first things I wanted to do as we began our ministry together was to get a desk where I could study. We couldn't afford anything fancy, but I managed to find a little desk that needed a lot of work doing to it. I got it home and set about tightening all the screws and sanding it down. It had a lot of watermarks on the top, so I painted it solid black. That was my study desk. I'll never forget it.

I set the desk in the corner of our bedroom, placing a small lamp on it and the few study books I had in my library at the time. I still recommend to anyone beginning their ministry to do as I did – get hold of a good study Bible, Webster's Bible Dictionary and a concordance. I also recommend the book *The Spirit Himself* by Meyer Perlman, *Knowing the Doctrines of the Bible* by Ernest S. Williams and *Bible Doctrines* by P.C. Nelson. That may not sound like much, but if you will burn the midnight oil as I did, night after night, you will be surprised at what you will learn. For many nights I studied with my beautiful wife sleeping in the bed behind me. It just felt right.

Some might wonder why I decided to put my study in my bedroom instead of a corner of the living room. All I can say is that it just felt good for me to sit there in the corner with my books, reading, writing and studying with the help of the Holy Spirit, with my wife behind me asleep. We were together and we had our new beginning. Those moments are still very precious to me. I knew Doris was with me as I studied and prayed into the wee hours of the morning. I'll never forget those early days in Possum Kingdom and the start of a ministry that still continues after fifty-two years. Don't ever forget where you came from!

When we reopened the church three families showed up. We had a dozen people including children. This was quite exciting. But we lived by faith – there was no salary for a pastor; no income of any kind, in fact. This is what I mean about everyone needing a Possum Kingdom in their life. We were going to have to trust the Lord all the way. To trust Him that He was totally committed to looking after us and providing for our needs, like He promised in His Word. We did just that and we witnessed the hand of God in so many ways.

We could fill many pages with numerous examples, but here are just a few.

One evening a deacon from another church showed up at our front door. "I was praying," he said, "and God told me to take an offering to the new pastor." He handed me a $20 bill, which back then was a lot of money.

We also had an eleven-year-old boy called Jakie come to our door and give us four ears of corn. I knew he was from a big family of eleven, and that they were very poor, so at first I refused. But Jakie said, "You have to take it pastor, because I felt like you needed this and I want you to have it. I was praying and the Lord told me to bring it to you." I was so humbled. I graciously received his gift, thanked him, and he went on his way.

That evening we had services in the little church and Jakie came bounding up to me, very excited.

"I want to tell you something pastor," he said.

"Sure Jakie, what is it?" I replied. He told me:

"When I got home, a man pulled up in front of our house in a truck and honked his horn. He called me over and handed me a sack. In it was twelve ears of corn – one for everyone in the family and two for me!"

Wow! This may seem like a small thing, but God was showing us through Jakie's example how He could provide even the simplest things for His children.

Not long after this a family in a big car pulled up in front of our house. We didn't know them at all, so we went out to greet them. The man who was driving told me he was an officer in the Air Force and had been transferred from California to Florida.

"We are on our way there," he told me, "but the strangest thing just happened."

He explained that they were Christians. As they were driving along the highway, singing songs and praising the Lord together, God spoke to the man very clearly and told him to pull off the road into this little town and to find a small church there.

"I've never been here in my life," the officer told me, "but I followed the Lord's direction and we found you."

I wondered exactly what it was they were supposed to do now that they were here. Then the officer pulled out $20 and handed it to me.

"God told me to come here and give you $20 and to pray with you and your wife," he said. He and his family were so excited. They praised the Lord and prayed with us, then they got back in their car and took off. We were just as excited as they were. As I've mentioned, $20 was a significant gift.

We were located about twelve miles off the main highway, but it seemed that God always had different people traveling down that road whom He impressed upon to pass through our little town. And then there were more children and more people from other churches who stopped by to pass on gifts or offerings.

Through it all, we were intentional about remaining thankful. Each time someone brought us a gift or an offering I wrote it on a large calendar, on the specific day we received it. The tens, the twenties, all were recorded.

Even though, in the beginning, we hardly had anyone attending the church, and the tithes and offerings were between just four and six dollars a week, somehow we always ended up with no less than $250 per month – which came from all kinds of different people from different walks of life. It was amazing to see how God met our needs without us asking or begging.

I will never forget one day when I was down town, walking in front of a store, and a man came staggering towards me. He was as drunk as anyone I had ever seen. He fixed his eyes on me and lurched straight for me. My first thought was, "Oh no, this guy is going to ask me for money, and I don't have any. I really don't need this today!"

Sure enough, when he got in front of me he stopped me and then reached out his hand. But then he said, "I don't have any idea why I am doing this, but I felt like I'm supposed to do this for you. He reached in his shirt pocket, pulled out a five-dollar bill, thrust it into my hand, and then staggered on down the road. I thought, "Just as the ravens fed Elijah, I guess God has his 'ravens' to feed us too. He takes care of us. He is a great God!"

The months passed by and God provided for us without fail. Then I found out that we were going to be parents. Doris was expecting our first child and she was sick a lot. I would often lead the Sunday morning service by myself as she suffered with morning sickness. Now we began trying to save some money for the baby.

One morning at the end of the service, after everyone had left, I counted up the tithes and offerings. It came to just four dollars and a couple of cents. I went into the parsonage. Doris got up and asked, "How are things?"

"Oh, great!" I replied. Secretly I was thinking, "We only have four dollars and we're trying to prepare to have a child. We have a big need! What am I going to do?"

Reading the look on my face, Doris asked, "Is everything okay?"

"Yes," I said. "I'm just going out – I'll be back in a while."

"Are you going to buy lunch? We need something to eat and we don't have any food!"

"Yes," I said again. "Don't worry, we are going to eat well."

With that I set off walking for the grocery store. I'd previously had a car – an Aero Willis – but the car payment was $12 per month, so I'd had to sell it.

Doris and I both loved lime sherbet. When we dated, we would always go and get a lime sherbet together, but since it was something of a luxury we hadn't eaten any since we'd been married. That day I went to the store and bought four dollars' worth of lime sherbet, which in those days was about two gallons. I couldn't think what else to do!

I returned home and Doris met me in the kitchen.

"Did you buy lunch?" she asked.

By this time I was having a real pity party with myself. God had been faithfully meeting our needs and I had no reason to believe He wouldn't continue to do so, but we are only human and that day I'd hit a roadblock in my faith. Sometimes we all go through similar things as our faith is stretched.

I slammed the sherbet down on the table and sat down. The sack burst open and I said, "We are going to eat lime sherbet and die!"

Doris gave me a strange look. I stared back at her. This was our lunch. I was as serious as a person could be and feeling really sorry for myself.

"If we're going to starve, we might as well start by eating lime sherbet," I reasoned.

Then we both started laughing. We stood there in the kitchen, with the lime sherbet sitting on the table, and thought how ridiculous we must look. Then we ate the lime sherbet anyway!

Without missing a beat – and despite the lime sherbet incident – God continued to supply our needs. People turned up at the house to bring us eggs, beans, vegetables and fruit.

We made it through the Possum Kingdom season of our lives and ministry. Looking back, I would not do anything differently, nor take away any part of that experience. We grew so much, in so many different ways. We didn't know then that in just a few years we would be traveling the world, often preaching to thousands (as well as just a few). God had used this time to prepare our hearts and to grow faithfulness in us. He helped us to see that, regardless of how we react, He is always faithful and never fails.

CHAPTER 16

Living Generously

When God provides for the needs of His children He is teaching us a double lesson. First, that He is more than able and willing to meet all of our needs, and will always make His provision available to us. But secondly, through this, He also teaches us the way of generosity.

Our Father is a generous God, and as we grow in faith we learn to emulate Him. He makes us into generous givers too. We learn that, just as God often uses His people to deliver His provision to us, so too are we His provision to others.

In Malachi 3:10 God makes the following promise:

> *"'Bring all the tithes into the storehouse,*
> *That there may be food in My house,*
> *And try Me now in this,'*
> *Says the Lord of hosts,*
> *'If I will not open for you the windows of heaven*
> *And pour out for you such blessing*
> *That there will not be room enough to receive it.'"*

Jesus taught us the principle of generous giving in Luke 6:38, highlighting the abundance of God's blessing:

"Give, and it will be given to you: good measure, pressed down, shaken together, and running over will be put into your bosom. For with the same measure that you use, it will be measured back to you."

Just as numerous people have given generously to us, we have endeavored to be generous towards others. Doris and I have given cars and vans to young missionaries, numerous books to young ministers to start a wholesome library that will help them in their ministry, and cash offerings to young ministers with families starting out in their first pastorate.

I don't write this to brag in any way. The further we walk with God, the more we learn to hold lightly onto the things we possess. They are just resources to be used to build His Kingdom. Many times things were put into our hands just so we could give them to someone else in need. We were just the channel, which these things came through.

What is really amazing about all this is we soon learn that no matter how hard we try, we cannot out-give God. Whatever we give away at His command comes bouncing back to us in one way or another.

Just recently I was preaching again in one of the churches that we planted in Santa Marta, Colombia. While we were there the pastor recalled an occasion when we had sent him a gift offering one Christmas. At the time he didn't possess a pair of shoes and had been praying that the Lord would provide him with the funds to purchase a pair. The money we sent him was the exact amount he needed to buy himself a good pair of shoes. "I received this letter from Franklin and Doris," he said, "with the correct amount of money I needed. I knew God had heard my prayer."

This was several years ago. At the time we had no idea he was in need. All we knew was that God spoke to us, told us to send him a certain sum of money, and we were obedient. Now we were privileged to hear about the need that was met. What an awesome God we serve!

Once Doris and I were on the road and stopped for a visit at New Wine Church in Keller, Texas. The pastor there was Dewayne Tracy. We were preparing to leave for Québec, Canada, to start a tent crusade. We had some of the money to purchase the tent, but still lacked $12,000. We needed that money to complete the purchase and set up in Canada. Before the pastor preached, he asked if I would come up and speak for about five minutes, sharing with the congregation our plans for this next crusade.

There were around 100 people present. I did as the pastor asked and spoke about what we were doing and about our need for finances to pay for the tent. I sat down, the pastor preached, and the rest of the service went as usual.

At the close of the service, one of the church board members spoke to me. He told me that some visitors from Dallas were there that day, and they wanted to know exactly how much money we needed to finish paying for the tent. I told him and he went away.

After the service, the pastor called me into his office.

"The visitors who came today wrote a check to help you with your mission endeavor to Canada," he told me, handing me a piece of paper.

I looked at it and it was a check for the full $12,000 we needed. Needless to say, Doris and I we so happy. We spent several months in Canada, preaching in several provinces, and ran the tent crusade for thirteen weeks.

What can $10 do for you?

We pastored a church in Pawhuska, Oklahoma, just prior to entering full time missionary work in South America. While pastoring the church, we started a program for boys called Royal Rangers. We had between thirty and forty boys. Each boy had to bring $10 to buy themselves a uniform.

In due course, every boy had purchased a uniform apart from one – a ten year old named Homer Shaw. Homer had several siblings and his family really didn't have enough money to live on. Our hearts went out to him when we realized that every boy had a uniform, apart from Homer. So Doris and I bought him the $10 uniform. He was so proud of it and it made him very happy. He was excited to be a part of the group and to not look like an oddball whilst everyone else was in their uniform.

Later, when we moved to South America we lost track of this young man and his family.

We no real idea of how this simple gesture had impacted this boy's life. We'd just purchased him a $10 uniform. But every now and then we began to hear from him. He would write to us overseas and tell us what he was up to. As the years went by, he was writing to tell us that he'd gotten married and had a great job and was doing well.

Then, on the occasion of his fiftieth birthday, I received a phone call from Homer. He asked if he could meet Doris and I in a small town just south of the Oklahoma border near Paris, Texas. He told me he had a gift for us because, he said, "I have never forgotten about the $10 that you spent to purchase me a uniform."

Doris and I hadn't seen him for forty years and we were delighted at the prospect of being able to meet up – and we would meet his wife too.

We arrived at the location and had lots of fun seeing him again and meeting his new wife. Then Homer passed me a set of keys. For what? Parked outside was a brand new Ford F-250 diesel truck. It had all the extras on it and, as if that wasn't enough, hitched to the back of it was a 35-foot RV travel trailer! The two items amounted to something in the region of $85,000 in value. Homer told us,

"I felt I had to buy this. But when I was buying it, I was telling God, 'I don't need anything like this!' He said to me, 'You're not buying it for yourself, you're buying it for Franklin and Doris.'"

Homer and his wife were so excited to give us the keys to this wonderful gift. I cranked up the diesel truck and we looked throughout the travel trailer. All the while Homer was saying to us, "I'll never forget what you did for me and I want to repay you by giving you this to help in your ministry."

As I drove that big rig away with Doris following behind in our car, I could hardly believe the goodness of our God. A $10 investment had reaped an $85,000 dollar reward!

We are serving a God of increase – a God who meets our needs and gives us more than enough. As you read this book, I want you to know that there is a God in Heaven who cares for you, just as He cares for us. He cares about the small things that you do for Him. He is mindful of you. When you give obediently on His behalf, He gives back to you thirty, sixty, ninety and sometimes even ten-thousand-fold what you gave away. You do your part and let God do the math! He is more than enough!

It would be impossible to tell you about all the wonderful gifts that have come our way. We were given a motor home in Borger, Texas. On another occasion, a brand new fifth wheel travel trailer that we took to Mexico and lived in for over two years. We were given a beautiful boat in Amarillo, Texas. We have been given motorcycles, cars, trucks, utility trailers and homes more than once.

Most of the time we sold these to raise the cash to buy more tents and build more churches. Regardless of the way they came, each gift was a tremendous blessing, not only to us, but also to the many people who otherwise would not have heard the good news of

Jesus and been saved. There are now church buildings in which new believers worship in many parts of the world because of the generosity of the hundreds of people we have crossed paths with.

There have been times when we have moved into a new city to plant a church and someone, somewhere had heard about our intentions and approached us to donate the land to build the church. That is a miracle beyond miracles, when the nationals in a foreign country give land, free and gratis, to build churches. All this is awesome.

I hope that you will live and learn that God is no respecter of persons and that He treats us all the same. He is as committed to providing for your needs as He is ours. If you have a need right now that you desperately need to be met, pray and ask Him and He will freely give it to you. Amen.

CHAPTER 17

How Far Can You Travel on $12?

We had just finished preaching a great two-week revival in Anson, Texas. It was the second time we had been there to conduct crusades. On the last night we decided to leave and travel to my mother's home in Haskell, Texas, which was just a few hours' drive away. That night, as I drove along with my wife and our two-month old daughter, I experienced a great encounter with the Lord. It never surprises me any more that God chooses to speak to us, but He frequently surprises me with what He has to say and how He chooses to do it!

It was the wee hours of the morning when I heard the voice of God, loud, clear and awesome! There was no doubt in my mind that He had just spoken to me and given me direction for our next assignment. He said,

"I want you to leave Texas, go to Tennessee and preach revival."

I was currently in West Texas – a very long way from the state of Tennessee; at least two days drive. However, I didn't question the Lord, I just accepted it; His presence was so powerful.

I reached over to shake Doris awake and said, "Honey, the Lord just spoke to me and said we are to go to Tennessee to preach revival." Her reaction expressed the words that I had already been thinking: "But we don't know anyone in Tennessee!"

It was true. I had never been invited to preach anywhere in that state at a church or any kind of crusade. We had never been there; we didn't know anyone there.

In due course, we arrived at my Mom's house in the early hours of the morning. Mom had been a pastor's wife and had helped my Dad pioneer a dozen churches, so she understood when I told her – having only just arrived there – that we were leaving and going to Tennessee!

There were, however, a couple of obstacles in the way. I had just $2 dollars left after we had finished paying all the bills for the crusade we had just completed. I assured my Mom that somehow we would get to Tennessee, $2 or not. Thank God for godly mothers. She didn't try to discourage me or tell me that this was nonsense. She just said that if I had really heard from God, then I should go for it.

"That's great son," she said. "You know the Lord will provide."

We spend the next day preparing to leave for our long road trip and planned to leave the day after that. At this point I guess I did a foolish thing in order to raise a tiny amount of additional cash. I took our car's spare tire to the local gas station and sold it for $5. Now I had $7.

That evening I was loading up my car when an elderly lady, a neighbor friend of my Mom's, came over and began chatting.

"Your mother told me that you're leaving for Tennessee," she commented.

"Yes, that's right," I confirmed.

"You know, I am on a fixed income," she told me, "But I want to give you $5 to help you on your road trip."

I expressed my thanks to her and gratefully received the money. Now I had a grand total of $12. The question is: *how far can you go on $12?* I didn't like to think, but I knew one thing for sure. However much you have, you can travel a long, long way on it when God is involved.

The next morning came and we were all packed and ready to go. We drove across the states of Texas and Arkansas and into Tennessee. We traveled solidly for two days before we finally pulled over at the side of the road. We slept in our vehicle, not having enough funds for a motel. Doris and I didn't buy any food either. Our only purchases were milk for the baby and gas for the car.

We finally arrived in Memphis, Tennessee. From there we headed north on Highway 51. I don't know why, except I was just following the leading of the Holy Spirit. I knew how Abraham must have felt when he set off to travel to Ur. When God says, "Go" you just go. We drove for the remainder of that day until we finally arrived in a town called Union City. The town beyond that would take us into the State of Kentucky.

Doris commented on this: "You know, if we go any farther, we'll be leaving the State of Tennessee!"

"Well, we can't go any farther anyway," I said, "because the gas tank is on empty and the baby is out of milk!"

God had said go to Tennessee and here we were, in Tennessee. We sat there for a moment and then I noticed a church across the road called First Assembly of God. I decided to go over there and see if anyone was around.

I knocked on the door. A lady opened it and told me she was the church secretary. I found this unusual because in those days, few churches had a full time secretary to run the church office, and this was in the middle of the day.

I explained to her that we were missionary evangelists and that we had traveled all the way across Texas and Arkansas to Tennessee. I wondered if it might be possible to speak to the pastor of the church. She told me,

"Go straight down this road for a few more miles and you'll reach another church called Old Republic Assembly of God. There's a Sunday School conference going on there. All of the pastors in this area are there today, attending that special meeting. If you go there now you'll find our pastor, and he is the president of this area. All the pastors should be there."

We made a quick detour to a nearby gas station to use the restrooms. We all got washed up and put on our good clothes. Just like Superman always changed his clothes in a phone booth, field evangelists like us often find ourselves getting changed in the restrooms at gas stations!

This is where the story gets really interesting. We drove down the road, found the church, and it was just as the secretary had told me. A meeting was in progress and one pastor was preaching from the pulpit. It was, I later found out, the pastor of the church in Union City.

We found a place to sit and began to listen to the message. At this point, however, one of the other men sitting on the platform jumped to his feet and approached the preacher.

"Excuse me for interrupting you pastor," he said, "but I have an announcement I must make right now!"

Slightly bemused the preacher stepped aside. The second man continued:

"As pastor of this church, I want to announce that we are starting a revival this Sunday with the couple who just walked through the door. I don't know them, but when they came in just now, God said to me, 'You are to start a revival this Sunday, with them.'"

With that he apologized once more to the speaker and sat down. I just sheepishly waved at him from where I was sitting. That afternoon, after the service had concluded, he took us back to his home and arranged a room for us. We started the revival meetings that Sunday and continued for the next two weeks. They were wonderful meetings!

During that time, other pastors in the area came and began to invite us to come and minister at their churches. All in all, we moved from church to church in that part of Tennessee for five months and God provided for all our needs.

God did great things through all the revival meetings, every night for five solid months. Many souls were saved and there were many miraculous healings. It impacted so many lives that even the Superintendent of the State of Tennessee, Brother Blythe, dedicated our baby, Wynelle, our first child, in one of the Tennessee district meetings.

Then we left to follow God's lead to Louisiana, and from there back to Texas. Later we returned to Tennessee to conduct more revival meetings. After all, now we had friends there!

God is awesome. If we will just be obedient to "go" where and when He tells us, then He will meet all our needs. Though faced with the circumstances, things may look impossible, but with God *everything* is possible! This is what happens when you follow the voice of God. He will speak if you will listen to what He has to say. Then you need to be obedient to His voice and you will be blessed and bear much fruit.

Packing barrels with R. D. Hays 1969

Leaving for Language School in Mexico

Language School

Clair Tromsness and Franklin preparing my first tent.

Franklin Leading the Sinners Prayer

Crusade Matamoros, Mexico

From tent crusade to church

Guatemala City, Guatemala crusade

Tent Crusade Quebec, Canada

Inside Tent Quebec

Tent Crusade Torreon, Mexico

Inside Tent

Tent Crusade Durban, South Africa

My Cuban Brother Eulogio Rivero

Central Church after crusade, Cartagena, Colombia

People coming to Church

The Best way they can find

Tent Crusade, Guadalajara, Mexico

Church Guadalajara

Returning to South America after Doris Healed of Cancer

Our Awesome Evangelistic Team

Doris & Lydia

Franklin-Costa Rica

Salvation, Cartagena, Colombia

Tent Crusade Costa Rica

Salvation & Healing Costa Rica

Managua, Nicaragua

Pastors North District, Colombia

Franklin & Pastors building Central Church, Cartagena

Central Church Completed

Crippled for 45 years, now healed

Franklin traveling across Andes Mountains

University Student saved in Puebla, Mexico

15 gang members baptized in Sincelejo, Colombia

Having Lunch in Andes, Mountains "Fresh Milk"

CHAPTER 18

Trusting God and Stretching Our Faith

After our extended crusade in Cartagena, Colombia, we were looking for a place to build a church. We were extremely blessed because we had already identified the man who would be the senior pastor of the new church – our dear friend Eulogio Rivero. He and his family had been exiled from Cuba and had arrived in Colombia. He was a quality man of God and we were very grateful that God had coordinated for us to work shoulder to shoulder in this pioneering work of the Lord.

We had been looking for some suitable land for some time. We were now going up and down the streets in Cartagena, trying to find empty buildings or empty lots on which we could build, but with no success. Eventually, we found a large piece of land where someone had started to construct a building, but had then run out of money. It was located right in the heart of the city, less than a block away from the main plaza. The reason we hadn't discovered it sooner was that a forest of tall grass and weeds had grown up to obscure it. In addition, the locals were using it as a garbage dump, so upon first inspection it just looked like a derelict lot.

After making some inquiries we found that we could buy the land for $5,000. It was a bargain – a miracle for prime, city center real estate. There was just one problem – I didn't have $5,000; nowhere near, in fact.

But believing that this was, in fact, the location that God had reserved for us, in faith we began the process of completing the paperwork necessary to secure the land. Then we just had to find the money to buy it.

A couple of days later Doris and I were in our bedroom, kneeling on opposite sides of the bed, both silently praying. We were asking God for direction regarding the land. After a while we both raised our heads off the bed and looked up at each other at the exact same moment. I said to Doris, "You know what? God just spoke to me and told me that we have a church right here in our home."

"That's wonderful," Doris replied. "He just said exactly the same thing to me. But what does that mean: 'You have a church here in your home'?"

We quickly realized that God meant the contents of our house. We had furniture; we had appliances; we had everything that we had shipped over to Colombia from the US. The people of Colombia loved to get hold of American furniture and goods. We also had barrels full of clothes and toys for our children.

"If we sold all of our things, we would have enough money to buy the land," I tentatively suggested to Doris.

"I feel the same way," she said, "and I am willing to do it."

I wanted to make sure that she really *was* willing and wouldn't regret it later. Doris assured me that it was fine.

"Okay," I said. "I'll put an ad in the local paper tomorrow, saying that we are selling all our possessions from the US."

A couple of days later, a man dressed in military uniform showed up at our house. I could tell from his uniform that he was a high-ranking officer.

"I've just been transferred to this city," he told me. "I only live a block from here, but we have no furniture in our house. How much do you want for it?"

I said, "$5,000."

He looked over our furniture for a short while and then said simply, "Okay, I'll take it. I'll give you the $5,000." He didn't try to bargain or get me to reduce the price; he just gave me the money and took away all our stuff.

You may wonder how we managed with no furniture in the house. Well, we just did without. It's amazing what you can do without if you don't have it. We were just thrilled because we now had the money to buy the land.

In due course we purchased it and I held the title deeds in my hand. With the help of Eulogio, we hauled all that trash off the property and began preparing it to house the new church.

Remember I said in an earlier chapter that we cannot out-give God? If we give to resource His Kingdom He will never leave us wanting. A few days later a man knocked on our front door and introduced himself as Gene Martin. Gene was the crusade director for Katherine Kuhlman's ministry, based in California.

I invited him into the house. Of course, we had no furniture in our home to entertain a guest. There was literally nowhere to sit! So I fetched a blue wooden bench that I kept in the back of my truck. We used it whenever we were carrying additional passengers with us. It swiftly became a makeshift "couch" for our living room.

The man looked amazed to see how we were living in this nice house, but with no furniture. He proceeded to tell us that he came bearing gifts. I asked what he meant. He explained that he worked for Katherine Kuhlman, who had a great TV ministry. We had read some of her books, but had never met her.

"Katherine was praying for South America," he informed us, "and all of a sudden the Lord dropped into her spirit the name 'Franklin Burns'. She asked us to find out who that was. We begin to investigate and ask missions organizations if they knew of a Franklin Burns. Eventually we found out that you were a missionary here, planting a church."

"Yes, that's right," I said, utterly amazed. "That's why we are here."

"As Katherine was praying," he continued, "God gave her your name and said to send you $5,000." At this point he reached into his attaché case and produced $5,000 in cash.

We were astonished and excited. In His grace God had spoken to someone we didn't even know and motivated them to seek us out, get on an airplane and come out to give us $5,000!

We gratefully received the money. But we didn't go out and buy new furniture with it, if that's what you're thinking. We used that additional $5,000 to finish the construction of the church building to seat several hundred people.

* * *

The first service we had in the new building was held on a Sunday afternoon. God was incredibly gracious. People came from everywhere and crowded into the building. We began to pray for people and in that very first meeting, a man who hadn't walked in almost five years jumped up and began to run around glorifying God.

Many years later, a great number of pastors have been a part of that church and have been sent out to plant other churches throughout the country. The children of many of these pastors are traveling the world, singing, ministering and spreading the gospel – including one of ours.

How humbling – God used us to plant the seed, which has grown into a mighty tree that has produced much fruit. Now the fruit has multiplied into other nations.

We visited there just recently to celebrate the church's 40th Anniversary. Brother Ripoll is the pastor there now. I was privileged to baptize him when he was just a teenager. Our dear friend Pastor Eulogio Rivero has gone on to be with the Lord. Today this church has a vision to plant at least another 200 churches. Thank God for His precious provision!

PART FOUR

The Blessing Of
Divine Protection

CHAPTER 19

Trusting in God's Protection

*"Though I walk in the midst of
trouble, You will revive me;
You will stretch out Your hand
Against the wrath of my enemies,
And Your right hand will save me."*
(Psalm 138:7)

One of the greatest weapons in our enemy's armory is fear. He tries very hard to intimidate us, to undermine our faith and make us afraid of stepping out in obedience to God, or take risks in faith – trusting that the Lord will be there to support us. Fear is a major stumbling block to pioneering evangelism: what if we don't get the resources we need? What if no one comes to our crusade meetings? If they do come, what if no one gets saved? Or healed? What if the locals don't like what we are doing and attack us?

The ramifications of fear-filled thinking are endless. Which is why so much of Scripture is filled with promises of God's protection. Knowing that we have a Heavenly Father who is more committed to protecting us than we are ourselves, robs fear and intimidation of their power.

It is all captured and summed up in the beautiful verse that reads,

"There is no fear in love; but perfect love casts out fear..." (1 John 4:18)

Over the years we have been incredibly blessed as, time and again, God has shown Himself to be ever-present with us, and a faithful protector of His servants. He is the One who is able to bring peace in the midst of the storm, but also in the ordinary ups and downs and challenges of everyday living.

Once, when Doris and I were preaching at revival meetings in West Texas, the daughter of the pastor we were working with came home from school in tears. Her dad asked her what the problem was.

"The teacher made fun of me in front of the whole class because I'm a Christian," Charlene told him.

This had happened because the teacher had asked each student to write an essay on the most important thing in their life. She had written her report stating that meeting Jesus was the most important thing that had ever happened to her. In the essay she described how she had received Him as her Lord and Savior and how she had been filled with the Holy Spirit.

Each student was supposed to read their essay aloud to the rest of the class. But when it came to Charlene's essay, the teacher took it upon himself to read out her essay – with the sole intention of ridiculing what she had written. He made fun of her for talking about Jesus and being filled with the Spirit.

Doris and I gathered with her dad around Charlene and prayed for her. We assured her that she had done exactly the right thing in celebrating her faith and her relationship with the Lord. Because of that, God would take care of her and so she shouldn't worry or be afraid.

It certainly hurts to be ridiculed and embarrassed in front of a group of our peers. People may well laugh at us for our faith, or think that we are stupid. But it is important that we stand our ground and refuse to allow the enemy to intimidate us and fill us with fear.

The next day, as Charlene set off for school, we assured her that the Lord was with her and to not worry. That afternoon she came home late. Her father was a little concerned about this, because she always came home on time, but when she finally arrived home she was grinning from ear to ear.

"You're not going to believe what happened to me today," she informed us.

She told us that as the teacher dismissed the class, he asked her to stay behind because he wanted to talk to her. Then he said he wanted to ask her some questions. Charlene thought, "Oh no, here we go again!" But the teacher had a different agenda.

"Charlene," he began, "last night I read your essay over and over again. I even got out a Bible I own, that hasn't been read for a long, long time, and began to read it. Your essay touched my heart. That has never happened before, so I just kept on reading it again and again."

At this point Charlene noticed tears running down the man's cheeks and dripping onto her paper.

"Last night," he continued, "I accepted Jesus Christ as *my* Lord and Savior and I began to speak in a language I had never spoken before."

Charlene looked at him in amazement.

"I was overwhelmed by the power of the Holy Spirit," her teacher said. "Thank you for writing what was in your heart. It made a difference in my life and impacted me so much that I'm now a different person! I want to ask you to forgive me for what I did to you yesterday, but also thank you from the bottom of my heart for standing your ground and speaking up for what you believe."

He thanked her again and then asked her if she would pray for him to continue to grow in the Lord. We give glory to God because of miracles like this. Because of a young girl's commitment to the Lord, a soul was saved.

Allow me to tell you about another crusade, this time in Sincelejo, Colombia.

The crusade was in full swing and we had been preaching every night for some time. We were really excited about the results we were seeing, with many salvations and miracles of healing. But on one particular night, a group of around twenty-five young men turned up at the meeting with ambitions not just to cause some disruption, but to inflict bodily harm.

They came armed with clubs and rocks and forced their way through the assembled crowd, shoving people out of the way, even hitting and knocking people down who didn't move quickly enough.

I had spotted them from the platform, outside the perimeter of the crusade. My truck was parked out there and they began beating on it. Then they plowed up the middle of the crowd, screaming, hollering and throwing rocks. One rock came whizzing through the air towards Doris, who was playing her accordion. I thanked the Lord that it hit the accordion and not her.

Eventually they were right up at the edge of the platform. Their message was pretty straightforward and simple: they were going to drag me off the stage and kill me! Silently I prayed and asked God for His help.

I want you to understand what an awesome God we serve! He immediately spoke to me – though what He said came as a great surprise. Ideally, I would have liked God to tell me to rebuke these men and command fire from Heaven to fall upon them! But that's not the way God works. God operates in peace. He is the One who can still any storm. So rather than rebuke them, God said to me,

"Speak My peace over them."

My initial reaction to this was, "Speak peace? I need something a little stronger than that, don't you think Lord?" God spoke to me again:

"Tell them, 'Peace. Be still.'"

I obeyed God's command and spoke with a loud voice through the PA system, in Spanish, *"Tengan paz"* – "Peace, be still". To my amazement, this angry mob froze in their tracks and none of them moved. As the presence of God was manifest in greater measure, peace flooded through my being too and any fear I had drained away. I had a revelation of how God's peace is the strongest weapon in the world – so much more powerful than violence.

This was an open-air crusade and some of the men helping us had already dug the trenches around the site that would later be filled to make the foundations of our new church building. That day it had been raining relentlessly and the trenches had been filling up with water – as much as four feet deep in places. As I spoke out, "Peace, be still," the leader of this gang – a young man named Livardo – just fell backwards and went splat into one of the deepest trenches.

I sat down on the edge of the platform and said to the rest of the group, "You guys come here now!" They all came forward sheepishly. There were no longer expressions of hatred and violence on their faces – they hung their heads and looked ashamed as if I had spanked them! It was the power of God, interceding for us.

They pulled Livardo out of the water and brought him to speak to me.

"Why are you doing this?" I asked him.

"Mario, our leader, sent us," he told me. We didn't know this Mario, but apparently he led a communist group who were vehemently opposed to Christian activity. He had given them instructions to put a stop to this new church being built and to end the crusade. But now they had been arrested by the power and presence of God, and every single one of them asked if I would pray for them.

I prayed and the Lord touched each one. After that they came along to the crusade every night. They had come with the intention of tearing down and destroying, but had encountered a higher power!

Right near the end the evening, near midnight, our pastor for the new church, Agustín, brought another man to see me. He introduced himself:

"I am Mario," he said. "I'm the leader of the group of men who came to stop your crusade. We came from our base in the mountains, intent on putting a stop to the construction of this church."

Despite his strong-arm tactics, Mario was a highly intelligent man who spoke five languages and had been well educated abroad. He had been present all along, but was observing his gang from a distance.

"I was watching my men," he told me, "when I saw one of the greatest manifestations of power I have ever witnessed. I have been searching all my life for such power. What was that?"

Another of our pastors, Ramos, responded:

"That is the power of the Holy Spirit. This is what serving Jesus, the Son of God, is all about."

Immediately Mario fell to his knees. "I want that power!" he said. "I want this person in my life!"

Right there and then we were privileged to share with him the saving grace of Jesus Christ – how He died for our sins and rose again, exalted to the right hand of Father God where He remains, making intercession for us. Mario gratefully accepted Jesus as His Lord and Savior before going on his way.

The next evening Mario was back.

"I want the power of the Holy Spirit, like I witnessed last night," he told me.

We prayed for him and he was baptized in the Spirit. Then he told us, "I am going to be an evangelist to my own people in the mountains." The last we heard of him, he was sharing the Gospel with many of the tribesmen who live throughout the mountain regions of Colombia, with great results.

Of the rest of the group, I was privileged to baptize fifteen of those men in the waters of the Caribbean Sea. Five of them went on to become pastors of churches that we planted! Some years later, Mario returned from his own missions activities, moved to the city of Barranquilla, where we were living, and became my secretary, sending correspondence courses out to those asking for Bible study material. God told us to "go and make disciples". It is such a privilege, not just to see people saved, but also to see them grow and mature in Christ. This is what it's all about.

There stands a church in Sincelejo today that has planted many other churches. Thanks be to God that the reality of His divine protection drives out all fear and allows the work of building His Kingdom to continue.

CHAPTER 20

"I Am With You Always"

Matthew 28:29

Once, when we were living in the city of Cartagena, Colombia, we needed to travel to the neighboring city of Barranquilla to help some new missionaries who were starting a work there and were just settling into living in the area. It was on this journey that the truth of God's Word was reinforced to us once again – that the Lord is with us always and He will never forsake us or leave us alone.

Our journey to Cartagena was a routine one, and we stayed there for several days before leaving to return, as our girls needed to be back in school. But on our journey home we encountered trouble like you would not believe! We were totally unprepared for the chaos we were about to be plunged into.

On the road from Barranquilla to Cartagena we needed to pass through a town called Luruaco. It was about halfway between the two cities. We had no idea that while we had been in Cartagena there had been a serious uprising in that town because several people had died due to a contaminated water supply. People called it a "strike" of the local workers – but in developing nations that word carries completely different connotations than in the US. It normally involves a great deal of violence and destruction.

As soon as we entered the outskirts of the town we knew something was terribly wrong. We got about halfway through the town when we suddenly encountered hundreds of people. One group had tied ropes around a large tree, pulled it down, poured gasoline over it and set it alight. Now they were dragging it down the road towards us, engulfed in flames.

There were three vehicles in front of us – each of which was desperately trying to turn around. There was a Jeep just ahead of us with an entire family in it. They were surrounded by a mob of people. Another group had surrounded a different car and rocked it backwards and forwards until they managed to roll it right off the road and down a hillside. Also in front of us was a young girl in a car by herself. They next thing I knew, the mob had surrounded her car and also rolled that off the road so that it went bouncing out of control down the steep hill.

We were in our pickup truck – Doris and I and the girls – all in the front bench seat. I was doing everything I could to get it turned around so that we could escape this madness and get to safety. Hands were literally grasping at the truck as I eventually managed to find some space and we got away with tires squealing.

But it was a case of out of the frying pan and into the fire. When we retraced our route back through the town we discovered that dozens of people had stacked up boulders in the middle of the road near the edge of town. There was no way to get out.

When I say "boulders" I don't mean small rocks – these were each a couple of feet high. As we approached this makeshift roadblock I slowed, but then saw people lined up on either side of the road. Effectively they had built a barricade and were just waiting, large rocks in their hands, to pound any vehicle that came near. Again we watched in horror as vehicles in front of us were stopped, turned over, and rolled down the steep ravines either side of this mountain road.

Although the angry crowd was screaming at us to halt, I knew it would be a terrible mistake to stop at this moment. I made it appear as if I intended to stop, slowing as I geared down my truck, and then I told Doris and the girls to brace themselves and to hold up their schoolbooks to protect their faces. I dropped into a lower gear then hit the gas and accelerated that truck with all power it could muster.

I hit the barricade at speed and we somehow literally catapulted right over it, landing safely on the other side. Rightfully we should have just smashed into those rocks, but somehow God lifted us over. Incensed, the crowd began throwing rocks at us. Rocks came hurtling towards the windshield, though amazingly none landed on it, and I hit the gas hard to accelerate out of there. I knew there would be plenty more rocks coming, because people were lined up on that road for some distance. They pelted us and the rocks made a deafening noise as they bounced all over the truck and we rode over the ones that had fallen to the ground.

Finally, we escaped and got out of there. At a spot well away from the town I pulled over to check out what I expected to be extensive damage to our vehicle. Headlights knocked out, dents, rocks lodged in the radiator and more – at least that's what I expected. To my utter amazement, there was not a single light broken. Nor were there any dents on the vehicle. It was as if the hand of God had shielded our truck. It was just amazing. We escaped with absolutely no harm whatsoever and not one rock had landed on our windshield – a complete miracle. Once again we were grateful for the protection of the God who cares for His children.

Of course, we still had to get home to the city where we lived! There was no other road to get there, so I began to take back roads that I didn't even know existed. We drove alongside the river and through standing water, in places two or three feet deep. We crossed rocky streams and all kinds of terrain to get back to Cartagena. It took hours and hours to travel by this twisty backcountry route. We drove on roads that were barely recognizable as roads! But we kept going, all the while asking God to direct and guide us.

Finally, after many hours of traveling, we reached the highway that went out to the southern part of the city where we lived. I didn't even know there was a way to get to it from where we had come, but through the guidance of the Lord we found it. It was late and dark when we arrived home safe and sound. By this time the children were asleep in the front seat! We got into our home and Doris and I just stood there, giving thanks and praising God for His miraculous protection.

We sat and talked about what we had experienced that day. How God had shielded us and kept us from harm. About the poor people who were attacked and had their cars rolled into deep ditches. How we had managed to escape against all odds. We thanked God for His grace and mercy.

I still pray for God's protection wherever we travel in the world and never take it for granted. God shows Himself to us over and over again. This is part of the reality of being called by the Lord. He calls us, sends us out, and we go in obedience. And where the Lord sends, He protects. We may encounter hardships and dangers, but the Lord is always in control.

God's promise to never leave us is as true for you today as it is for us. If you remain faithful to Him and rely upon His Word, you will be full of His peace and power. Give glory to God, for He is with you always and forever.

CHAPTER 21

God Can Use The Smallest Things

Many people think of God as very remote and distant, disinterested in our daily lives. Nothing could further from the truth! God is *so* mindful of every detail of our lives that often He uses the smallest, seemingly insignificant things to bring about His purposes in our lives, and to keep His promise to protect us and bless us.

After we had been based in Mexico for some time, we left there to head into Central America and the country of Nicaragua. We had plans to run a citywide crusade in the capital city of Managua. A missionary already resident there had prepared the location ahead of our arrival and had erected a small tent and a platform in front of it.

We had no way of knowing that this tent was going to be way too small for the crowds of people that God was going to send our way on this particular mission. We also had no way of knowing that we would once again be blessed and thankful to know God's awesome protection on the journey to get there!

It was a time of political unrest and the day that we arrived at the border of Nicaragua it was swarming with military personnel. It was a cold, rainy day, which was very unusual for Central America. All the soldiers were wearing heavy clothing and field jackets. At any border we always had go through the mandatory vehicle search procedure, so that the authorities could check we weren't trying to smuggle anything in.

At that time they were particularly concerned about people bringing in weapons or ammunition – anything that might contribute to the war that was currently erupting in their country. At that time, the leader of the nation was President Somoza. A militant faction had started in one part of the country led by a man called Sandino. His followers, the Sandinistas, were growing in number and protesting about many things that were happening in their nation. In due course this unrest would result in full-scale civil war.

We had heard rumors to this effect already, but had decided to go to Nicaragua anyway in response to the call of God. Although it might be dangerous, we were sure that having called us, God would protect us. Nevertheless, we were surprised to see the strength of the military force that was spread throughout the region and on the borders.

As we drove up to the checkpoint a soldier came over to inspect our vehicle and took our visas. One man, who said he was in charge of that part of the operation, said he would check my truck to see what I was bringing into the country. Our family had just recorded a gospel album with a group called "The Galileans" and we had several boxes of albums that we planned to distribute at the crusade. Each box had 50 LPs in it.

Thinking he was onto something out of the ordinary the solder became animated. "What is in these boxes," he demanded. I guess he thought we might be stupid enough to bring in boxes of ammunition or something else in full view.

"They're just LP records," I told him.

"I want to see one," he said.

"Sure," I replied.

He opened up one of the boxes, pulled out a record, and took a good look at it. On the back of the sleeve was our family picture and a picture of the Galileans. On the front was a picture of the snowcapped mountain *El Volcan Popocatépetl* that is located right outside Mexico City. I had taken the picture myself from our rooftop.

The soldier looked at me and said, "I like this record. Can I have one?"

"Of course you can have one," I replied; glad to give him a gospel album.

He unzipped his field jacket, looked around to make sure none of his colleagues were watching, and slipped it inside.

"You're now free to go," he told me. He turned to some other soldiers and said, "This man has been checked, let him through."

I thought this was a great result. Not only were we free to go on swiftly on our way with the minimum of disruption, but I had given the man a gospel album too! We drove on into the country.

As we left the border this little incident quickly left my mind as thoughts turned to the crusade we would be running in Managua. In due course we had settled into the place we would call home for the duration of our stay and soon the meetings began. God blessed us and we saw outstanding results from the mission. Wonderful things were happening every single night and there were many salvations and miracles. Other missionaries in the area came in to help us cope with the big response from the local people and even the Galileans showed up to sing at this open air crusade. We preached to a congregation of around 5,000 people.

The civil unrest got worse and worse and boiled over into full-scale war. Things got so bad that soon everything in the city began to shut down. The Sandinistas had grown so strong that they overthrew the Somoza army in the main city. They took over the airports, the railroads and the buses. They took over all radio and television communications. They were now in control.

We continued preaching at the open-air crusade in spite of all this. Many times, as our meetings continued, we heard gunfire in our vicinity. Occasionally, people witnessed bullets flying over their heads. One time, as Doris and I were standing to one side of the platform, we heard the crack of gunfire and heard a bullet whistling by nearby. Eventually things became so bad that everything needed to be shut down. It wasn't safe to continue and people were afraid of losing their lives. We did not want anyone to be killed and it was too risky to have so many people gathered together in one area.

We were told by other missionaries, however, that there was now no way to get out of the country, since the Sandinistas had taken over so the entire transport infrastructure. No one could get in or out. The Sandinistas even announced on radio and television that if anyone so much as attempted to leave the country, they would be shot on sight, no questions asked.

After a few days, a group of us gathered together in the basement of Kenneth Smith's house – one of the other missionaries. We were talking and praying about what to do and how we could get out of the country. What was going to happen? How long would we be trapped there? How could we continue with our missions work?

In the midst of all this debate, God suddenly spoke to me very clearly.

"I want you to leave in the morning."

This was very unexpected! I stood up and addressed the other missionaries. "The Lord just told me to leave the country in the morning," I said. They were amazed.

"You can't do that!" someone protested. "You've heard what they've said on the radio and TV. Anyone approaching the borders, trying to leave, will be shot."

"All I can say is what I've heard," I responded. "I know I heard God clearly telling me to leave in the morning, so I'm taking my family and going."

I think they thought I had lost my mind. The following morning we packed all our things into the car and got ready to leave. I had a Suburban at the time. The only problem was, it was painted olive green. It wasn't a choice of color I'd have been happy with if, when I set off, I knew I was headed into a war zone! It was the exact same shade as all the military vehicles.

When we were ready to go, we said goodbye to all our missionary friends, got into the Suburban and drove off. They all stood in the road waving, probably thinking it was the last they'd see of us. Thanks be to God that wasn't the case.

We had to pass through a number of smaller towns on our way to the border. At the first one, we spoke to some soldiers who said that the war was really bad in the next town. When we reached that town, in fact there wasn't much happening. There were plenty of military personnel all over the place, but it looked as though things were on hold. We were the only vehicle on the road and we passed through there without incident.

Just as we were leaving the town limits, however, I noticed in my rearview mirror a bulldozer pulling into the middle of the road. They obviously planned to cut up the road and make it impossible to pass through. We had made it out of there with seconds to spare. It was nothing short of a miracle.

Eventually, we reached the border where we wanted to pass out of the country. The Immigration office was located to one side of the bridge that spanned the border. I parked up, walked into the immigration office and laid our passports on the official's desk. He immediately jumped to his feet.

"What are you doing here?" he demanded.

"I need you to stamp our passports because we are going to leave the country," I told him.

"You know you can't do that," he said. "You cannot leave the country!" He gestured out of his window. "Do you see all those soldiers up there on the bridge?" he asked. I looked and, of course, there were soldiers everywhere, all bearing weapons.

"They have orders to shoot anyone who tries to get onto the bridge," he said.

"I want you to stamp our passports," I persisted, "and give us permission to go ahead and leave."

"No," he responded. "I will not be a part of your death." He shoved the passports back across his desk.

"Take these and go. I will not stamp your passports and I will not be responsible for you."

"Okay," I said. I went back out to the Suburban and spoke to Doris. "What did he say," she asked.

"That we are free to go," I replied.

Doris had traveled all over the world with me without asking lots of questions about what we were doing, where we were going or why. She is an amazing example of quiet trust in the Lord. She believes God and she believes me, her husband. We had been through many different countries together and we knew that God always had His hand on us.

"Just pray that we are going to cross that bridge," I said to her. "God told us to leave this country this morning and I know He has a plan."

I don't know what the average idiot does in a situation like this, but I know what someone who has heard the voice of God does. He moves forward in trust. Remember that often God uses the seemingly insignificant to bring about His purposes? God's timing is impeccable, because now was the time He decided to use one.

I began to drive slowly towards the bridge. As I approached the edge, a soldier stepped into the road in front of me, raised his weapon and hollered at me to stop. He was extremely angry. I stopped. He walked up to our car. He had his helmet on, pulled down so that his face was in shadow.

"Who are you?" he yelled. "What do you think you are doing? Why are you trying to get onto the bridge?"

I opened my mouth to speak – to say, "I need to leave the country," but before I could get a word out, the soldier began to smile. He looked me up and down, looked around our vehicle, and then said,

"Hey! Do you have another one of those LPs you gave me?"

I realized he was the man who had been in charge of vehicle checks the day we had entered the country. On this day – the day God had told us to get out of the country – he was the man in charge of the bridge.

"What are you doing here?" he asked again, no longer shouting.

"I really need to cross the bridge and get out of the country," I told him.

"It was nice to see you again," he said. Then he stepped back and yelled to the other troops, "Let my friend cross the bridge!"

The soldiers stepped aside and Doris and I drove across the bridge. I don't think we dared breath until we were safely on the other side and passing out of Nicaragua. God had miraculously intervened and protected us. It was mind blowing to think that He had set in motion a plan, for our benefit, that involved a vinyl LP that would be our ticket to get both in and out of the country. What an awesome God we serve!

CHAPTER 22

God Has A Bigger Plan

"And we all hear these people
speaking in our own languages
about the wonderful things God has done."
(Acts 2:11)

In the early 70s we traveled to a small fishing village on the Magdalena River in Colombia to pioneer a new church and erect a building for the people of Santo Tomas. We saw the hand of God moving with signs, wonders and miracles like we had not witnessed for some time.

It was difficult for us to find a suitable location in that area, but a family by the name of Zapata, who had lived there all their lives, said that they wanted to contribute to our ministry and help us with our plans. They donated a prime piece of property to us, right on the main highway, where we could run a crusade and build a church. This in itself was an outstanding miracle, since land is such a precious commodity in these countries.

We began laboring on the land to prepare it for the construction of the new church. God gave us great favor in that place. The mayor of the town showed up with a pickup truck full of vegetables, fruit and other food to feed us and the people who were working alongside us. We had never witnessed such an expression of love in any of the towns where we had already worked. We became expectant of a tremendous move of God amongst the people of Santo Tomas.

During the preparation we were contacted by a group of young people from the US, mostly teenagers, who wanted to come out to Colombia on a mission to do personal evangelism. They had heard about our ministry and wanted to come and work with us. We were always delighted to received additional helpers, so we said yes and in due course a team of young people arrived. They were very excited and really on fire for God, eager to serve the Lord.

It so happened that in the remote fishing village where we were based the locals had never seen Americans before and were not at all familiar with the English language. Added to that, none of the teenagers from the US spoke Spanish. It was therefore necessary to create teams of two or three, pairing up American kids with Colombian ones, so that each team would have an interpreter.

In due course, groups of young people went out and began going from house to house doing evangelism, telling people about Jesus – the English kids speaking through the Spanish youth.

One of the young ladies was called Donna. She was seventeen years old. On one day, when everyone had paired up and all the teams had gone their way to witness up and down the sandy streets of the village, she was somehow left behind with no one to go with.

Needless to say, she was quite upset about this. So she came to me and begged me to let her go down one particular road to invite the people there to come to the crusade we were planning. She really wanted to tell people about Jesus.

I assured her that there was no way I was going to let her go off on her own. She was a beautiful young American girl in a foreign country, in a remote village that had never seen young people like her. She didn't speak a word of the language and would be extremely vulnerable and unable to defend herself, should anything happen.

I kept on saying no, but Donna was extremely persistent.

"Franklin, please let me just go down this one road," she pleaded. "I promise I will not get off this road – I'll stay right here, knocking on doors and witnessing."

"But Donna," I reasoned, "you don't speak Spanish. No one is going to understand you. And I can't let you go without a chaperone."

She wouldn't listen.

"Some way, somehow, God will help me to speak to these people," she said. "Please let me go!"

I kept on saying no and Donna kept on pleading. In the end, against my better judgment, I gave in and said, "Okay Donna, go down this road only, and just knock on doors. Don't go inside any of the houses, even if they invite you in." All of these kids had paid their own way to travel from the US to Colombia and I guess I didn't want to disappoint her.

"Okay," she said, "I promise."

I let her go, but made up my mind to check on her very shortly. First I needed to take a quick look to see how the other teams were doing. I drove up and down the village in my truck a couple of times, looking to see what the teams were up to, then told myself it was time to get back and see how Donna was doing.

I arrived back in the road where I'd left her – and where she had promised to stay – and there was no sign of her. I drove up and down that road several times and she was nowhere to be seen.

I jumped out of the truck and began to run from house to house. I looked for some of the local kids on the street, to ask if they had seen her. It was common for the visiting teenagers to attract the attention of the local kids, who would follow them around wherever they went. But I couldn't find any kids and there was no Donna.

By this time I was highly frustrated and very concerned. I was angry at myself. I had known better than to allow this and I'd let it happen anyway. Now I was frantically running up and down the road trying to find Donna. I was looking everywhere when, all of a sudden, I rounded a corner and there she was. Technically she was still "on the road" liked she'd promised, but she had gone down one of the side streets.

I saw that she was busy speaking to a group of eight fishermen. The fishermen in that area were hard working guys, shirtless, tanned by the sun, with nets slung over their shoulders. They were on their way to the Magdalena River, just down the road.

As I approached, I noticed that they were all stood there attentively listening to Donna telling them how Jesus died on the cross for their sins; that He rose again and ascended into Heaven; that He loved them.

As I listened to her message of salvation and the love of God, as good as it was because she was speaking passionately from her heart, I was thinking, "These people don't have a clue what she is saying."

I decided that she needed some help and that I would step in and begin to interpret for her. But before I had chance Donna said to the men,

"Please throw off your nets, kneel down and raise your hands towards Heaven. Begin to ask Jesus Christ to forgive your sins and cleanse you from all unrighteousness. Tell Him how much you love Him and want Him as your Lord and Savior."

Right then, I saw with my own eyes, eight fishermen who knew not one word of English, simultaneously throw down their nets, fall to their knees, and raise their hands in prayer.

These folk had never had any exposure to the gospel. They knew nothing of prayer or calling on God. But they all knelt, looked to the heavens, and I heard them begin calling upon the name of Jesus in their own language, asking Him to save them, forgive them, cleanse them and make them whole. Each man received Jesus as Lord.

Now Donna noticed me standing by her.

"Oh, Franklin," she exclaimed. "I need your help."

"You don't need my help Donna," I told her. "God has intervened."

God had done an incredible miracle. Speaking from the heart Donna had shared the good news in her own language and the fisherman had heard it in theirs. I was reminded right away of the scene in Acts 2 when the Holy Spirit fell and people heard the message of the gospel in their native tongues.

Once again I was amazed by how God will work miraculously to fulfill His Word and touch the lives of those who are lost. We continued to evangelize that town for several weeks. We built a building and it was filled with people from the very beginning.

I was also extremely grateful that God put His protection around a young girl who was full of faith, determined to serve Him. God always protects His children!

Part Five

The Awesome Power Of Our God

CHAPTER 23

Supernatural Intervention

Time and again it has been impressed upon us, how awesome is the power of the God we serve. In previous chapters we have spoken about God's provision and protection. In the final few chapters of this book we want to recount some stories that give glory to God for His sheer awesomeness and power! It has been amazing to see how God will intervene supernaturally in situations where we need special help.

Entertaining angels unaware

We were back in the city of Guadalajara, Mexico to start a new work and raise up another new church. On this particular Sunday, after our morning service had finished, our family decided to go and have lunch together at the restaurant in the local Holiday Inn. We had our four-year-old granddaughter, Angelica, with us.

Soon after we'd finished lunch, Angelica was playing outside near the swimming pool and we suddenly noticed that her nose was bleeding quite profusely. Initially, I wasn't that concerned – just a simple nosebleed. We checked that she hadn't fallen or hit her head. Her nose just started bleeding for no apparent reason.

I became concerned when, after my wife, daughter and a couple of other ladies had attended to her, she was still bleeding. In fact, they got through five or six pool towels, each of which was soaked in blood. The bleeding showed no sign of abating.

Things suddenly took a serious turn when blood began coming out of Angelica's mouth too. I was sure it was going to go down her throat. We needed help – fast. I prayed.

"God, what is going on? What should I do? Where do we need to take her? Father, help me! I need help for my granddaughter."

As soon as I had uttered those words I heard someone approaching in a hurry from behind. I turned to see one of the largest Mexican men I'd ever seen in my life. He was not only broad and large, but also extremely tall. He marched straight over to my wife and daughter, who were still trying to help Angelica, reached down, and scooped her up in his arms.

To date, Angelica had never allowed herself to be picked up or cuddled by any stranger, so I expected her to get distressed and begin hollering. Instead she seemed to become peaceful and didn't murmur. The man turned to me.

"Where's your car?" he asked.

"Out front," I said.

"Let's go!" he said.

We all dashed out of the hotel to my car, with the huge Mexican following. When we got to the car, he handed Angelica to her mother, Wynelle, and she and my wife continued praying for her. At one point we had stopped praying but Angelica said, "Keep praying in tongues!" while we got in and he began to direct me.

"Go straight out of here and turn right now," he ordered.

I had absolutely no idea where I was going. Wynelle was still clutching Angelica. Something told me to run with it and follow orders. We went quite a way down the road when he said,

"Turn right here."

I did, and to my surprise I was looking at a small hospital. We pulled up on the front and all jumped out of the car. The big man marched through the front door. He didn't pause to speak to anyone at the nurses' station in reception, he just kept walking briskly. He called out to someone, "Get me a doctor!" and, as if he knew exactly where he was going, headed towards a room at the end of a long corridor. He went straight in and laid Angelica on a bed.

Almost immediately a doctor showed up and began to examine her nose. I could not believe how tranquil our granddaughter was. She was neither upset nor crying, but perfectly at peace. Shortly, the doctor told us that he had everything under control and she would be fine. At this point, the Mexican man turned to me and said, "I must go now!" and stepped out of the room.

Doris turned to me. "Honey, you could at least offer him a lift back to the hotel," she commented.

"Of course," I said. "I will do that."

I stepped out after him. I was surprised to see that the long corridor was deserted.

"Wow, that guy moved quick," I thought to myself.

I took off walking as fast as I could in order to catch him up. He had left just seconds before me, so I was sure I would find him. I went all the way to the exit at the front of the building, past the nurses' station. There was no sign of him. I asked a couple of people, "Have you seen the man who came in here carrying my granddaughter in his arms?"

"No," they said.

"Well, where did he go then?" I asked, puzzled.

The nursing staff looked equally puzzled at me.

"No one has come out here since you all came in" I was told.

"No, no," I insisted. "A very large, tall man just came out. He was just with us a moment ago and then left."

One nurse replied, "I'm sorry, but no one has come out. We would have noticed."

Thinking they must not have been looking I dashed out of the front door, across the small parking area and stood in the road, looking this way and that. There was no sign of the guy, who must have left on foot as he'd arrived in our car! Shaking my head I returned to the hospital room.

Angelica was now fine. The bleeding had stopped. The doctor was satisfied that it was nothing more sinister than an aggressive nosebleed, and that she was absolutely fine to leave.

Doris and I looked at each other and she said, "That had to have been an angel. He came from nowhere, picked her up and she was completely calm. He was only at the hospital with us for a few minutes and then he was gone. No one else saw him!"

"I guess we entertained an angel unaware," I said.

As the Bible tells us, often God will send angelic assistance to His children, but in a form that disguises their heavenly identity. It was the only explanation. How else could we explain how this man – unusually tall in stature for a Mexican – who had immediately taken charge of the situation, marched into the hospital like he owned it and got Angelica individual attention from a doctor, and yet brought such a sense of peace with his presence?

I thank God that there are ministering angels still around to take care of us! Amen.

It's a miracle!

Rosa Rubio was a fine Christian young lady and came from a Christian family who were very faithful to the church in the city of Guadalajara, Mexico. Rosa married a young man named Joel. He was working with me as a worship leader and in ministry planting new churches in that city.

Some time after they were married, Rosa announced that they were expecting twins and that she was about four months along. Everyone was delighted by this wonderful news. But as the pregnancy continued, Rosa began having a lot of complications. One day she went to see her pediatrician because she was bleeding severely and he immediate hospitalized her.

After monitoring her condition for several days in hospital, the doctor brought her some very bad news. He could not locate the heartbeat of the second child. He went on to say that he believed one of the children had died in the womb; therefore they were going to have to perform an abortion.

You can imagine how Rosa felt. She and Joel began to pray and seek God for help and guidance, so that they could make a decision. After praying, Rosa felt strongly in her spirit that she was going to be able to give birth to the other twin, who was still alive.

Dr. Manuel Perez was not in favor of this at all. He began to explain to Rosa that such an action could cause severe infection, possibly even cancer, and would endanger her life. He highly recommended the abortion of both children. Rosa's final decision was, "I'm not going to have an abortion. I am going to give birth to this child normally."

As I recount this testimony with you, I have before me two different sonograms. One sonogram shows that there are clearly two children in the womb. The accompanying medical report from Dr. Perez explains the severity of her condition and his recommendation of an abortion.

But I also have before me a second sonogram. This second one was taken after Rosa and Joel had prayed and after Rosa declared that she would give birth normally to her other child. Amazingly, the later sonogram clearly shows only one child in the womb. Dr. Perez told Rosa that this was nothing short of a miracle and could not understand what had happened.

"We don't know what happened to the dead child," the hospital staff told the couple. "You have been here in our care the whole time. We would have known if you had somehow lost the child, but the baby who died has simply gone. We can't explain it. The good news is that the other child is moving. Its heart rate is normal and it seems to be a perfectly healthy child."

I am happy to report that Rosa gave birth to a normal, healthy child without complications. The child is doing well and Rosa is fine too. The doctor recorded the occurrence of this miracle in his report. We all give glory, praise and honor to God for this outstanding miracle.

Rosa and Joel have continued to work with us for some time now and each time I hear them give their testimony in one of our services I can't help but think what an awesome God we serve and how He continues to be with us in times of trouble. He will never leave us nor forsake us. Put your trust in Him for he cares for you!

God speaks in mysterious ways

It was during the time when we were pastoring a church in Pawhuska, Oklahoma, that I heard the voice of God speak into my spirit and tell me to go immediately to a particular funeral home in the city.

I hesitated at first because it was 7 o'clock in the morning and I really can't say that I understood why God was prompting me to do such a thing. But I was obedient to His call. I dressed as quickly as I could and went immediately to the funeral home, only to find it closed with no one around. I sat there in my car praying and wondering what God had in mind. The Lord then immediately spoke to me again to go to the home of one of the brothers in the church. This time I really felt a real sense of urgency to get there as fast as I could.

When I got to his home, once again there was no one around. I knocked at the front door several times and there was no response. I walked around the house trying to see if there was any one around. I went to the back door and knocked and knocked again and still no one answered. I then pulled at the screen door and it came open. I tried the main door and that was unlocked too.

I guess in all my experiences as a traveling missionary, fear has never been one of my weaknesses, so I just headed into the house to see what was going on. I entered by the kitchen and began to call out this brother's name. All of a sudden I froze in my tracks. There he was, standing about six feet away from me, holding a .44 Magnum handgun, about to take his own life.

"No," I called out. "Don't do that! Please don't do that."

He hesitated. Then he looked up and pointed his gun straight at me.

I remember speaking to him and praying at the same time. I've always been told you can't have two thoughts at the same time – but here I was doing it. Slowly, I reached out my hand.

"Please give me the pistol. You don't want to do this," I said.

He looked at me and said emotionally, "I'm going to give it to you. I'm going to give it to you!"

I realized that his statement could be interpreted in more than one way! Was he going to hand me the gun or was he going to shoot me?! Thanks be to God he lowered his weapon and then turned it over to me.

Then he ran into his bedroom and fell down on his knees beside his bed. He began to weep bitterly, shaking and trembling. I got down on my knees beside him and was praying for him and unloading the pistol at the same time. I took those .44 Magnum bullets (that appeared to be as large as cannonballs) out of it and stuck them in my pocket.

We prayed for some time before he got up, sat on the bed, and began to tell me how, after serving for forty years in the same job, he had been dismissed. He was out of work and, I guess, felt that he had completely lost his identity as well as his livelihood. I realized that sometimes, though we may be a God-fearing person who loves the Lord and serves Him, sometimes we can be so devastated by the events of life that we can lose the closeness of our walk with the Lord if we don't seek to protect it. We are only human. That's why it is important to keep ourselves in a state of surrender to the Holy Spirit and allow Him to minister to us through life's ups and downs.

My friend told me to take the pistol home with me and not to give it back to him. I told him that when the time was right, we could talk things over. I continued to be his pastor for some time after that. I continued to pray with him, love him and to let him know I was there for him any time he needed me.

When I left the church to continue our ministry, I met with this man again. I asked if he was ready to take his pistol back and he assured me that everything was all right and that he had everything under control in his mind and spirit. I give him back his gun and he thanked me over and over again.

Then he asked me a question.

"How did you know," he wondered, "what I was about to do and why did you show up at my home at that precise time?"

I told him the story of how God had taken me first to the local funeral home, before directing me to his house. Why did God work in this way? Sometimes, in order to reveal His power to us, God needs to help us to be obedient to Him – and He does it step by step, leading us into His purposes. He knows best – He is God after all! – and it worked. The amazing thing is, God cared so much about this man that He orchestrated events in order to come to his rescue. This is the kind of God we serve – One who loves us dearly and is mighty in power. Praise God, because He is mindful of you.

CHAPTER 24

A New Jacket

We had been preaching a crusade in Puebla, Mexico, and were blessed to have our favorite singing group with us, the Galileans. At the close of the crusade we were able to buy some land with an existing building. We converted it to a church with Sunday school classes and living quarters for the pastor.

The crusade had lasted for several months. Then we were visited by a pastor from another city, Apizaco, Tlaxcala. It was about an hour and a half away. Tlaxcala is the smallest state in the country of Mexico, nestled high in the mountains. We were delighted to respond to Pastor Juan's invitation to come and hold a crusade and build a church there. It's what we love to do – go into new cities, towns and villages with no church, preach the good news about Jesus, and then teach and train the people.

One afternoon we arrived early at the crusade site to prepare ourselves for the people who would be coming from the town and surrounding area. This particular day, as we arrived, we noticed a man and his wife sitting on a wall. They looked as if they were waiting for us.

I walked over to say hello and the man asked me if I was the evangelist. I assured him I was. He then reached into his shirt pocket and produced an 8x10 flyer that had been distributed around the area announcing the crusade. It had been folded and kept in his pocket for some time and was kind of ragged. He pointed to the mountains way beyond the town and said to me,

"Do you see that mountain top?"

"Yes," I said.

"That's where we live," he explained. "On top of that mountain." He held up the flyer. "Someone in our village gave this to me. I didn't have a way to get here, so my neighbor brought us down the mountain as far as he could in his mule cart. Then another cart with a donkey brought us the rest of the way into the town. After that, a taxi driver who noticed that I was crippled and could not make it any further, helped us into his car and told us there would be no charge. He said he would take us to the address on the flyer – and that is exactly what happened."

I was amazed by this story and the effort the man had made to get to the crusade. Now, as he sat there, I noticed that one of his feet was twice the size it should have been. It was bandaged with nothing more than rags – and visible through the rags was an infection, with some blood was seeping through.

Another thing caught my attention. He was wearing only a thin shirt with a couple of buttons on it. We were all wearing heavy coats because it was so cold in those high mountains of Mexico. His wife was dressed a little better than him, but even she was not dressed adequately for the cold weather.

He sat there looking at me, clearly expecting something. Immediately my mind was filled with images from the third chapter of Acts. Peter and John went into the temple to pray and there was a man asking for alms. Peter said, "Silver and gold have I none, but such as I have, give I you." At that moment he reached out and took the man by the hand. The man leapt to his feet dancing and shouting, and even went into the temple shouting and dancing because he had been miraculously healed.

I realized that the book of Acts was still being written 2,000 years later by men and women of God! I realized that God is not finished with any of us yet. At that moment the man said to me, "We have come all this way from the mountaintop, arriving here early this morning, to sit here and wait for you."

My heart went out to him. At that moment my faith soared and I realized afresh that God still hears and answers prayers for a miracle. I bent over, took him by the hand and began to pray. The anointing of God came down like a bolt of lightning, and "struck" this man. He literally leapt to his feet. Then he exclaimed loudly,

"I couldn't walk. I haven't walked, I haven't worked, I haven't been able to do anything! But now I felt something go through my body like a bolt of electricity."

Then he began to run around the large, open field we had prepared for the crusade. He was running and stomping his feet. Eventually he came running back. He fell down on his knees and grabbed me by the hand. I told him, "No, stand up. It's not me! God has miraculously healed you." Indeed, he had been totally healed.

The blue and gold jacket

During this mission I had my sixteen-year-old nephew, David Stanley with me, who had come over from the States to work with us for a little while. He was part of a school program called Future Farmers of America or FFA. The FFA had given him a beautiful blue and gold corduroy jacket as part of the program. David was really proud of it and wore it all the time.

Just as the evening service was about to begin, I noticed that David wasn't wearing his jacket, so I asked him where it was.

"Where's your coat? It's so cold and windy here."

David had noticed the shabbily dressed, poor mountain man, with his long, shaggy hair and threadbare clothes. He told me,

"That man who had the crippled foot – I couldn't stand to see him without a coat, so I took mine off and gave it to him. He was so happy, he kept hugging me and thanking me over and over."

I was proud of my nephew. "David, that's awesome," I told him. "I know you loved that jacket, so it was a difficult thing you did. I know God will reward you for it."

A few nights later at another of our services I saw Pastor Juan and asked him if he knew what had happened to the man who had come from the mountaintop.

"He's right here," Juan told me.

I looked and I hardly recognized the man! He'd had his hair cut short and it was nicely combed and he was wearing better clothes. Beside him was his wife and their six children, all neatly dressed. I went over to him and then noticed he was proudly wearing David's blue and gold FFA jacket which had the words, "Hugo, Oklahoma" in gold letters. He was smiling and looked as healthy as a man could be. The first thing he said to me was,

"Pastor Franklin, after I got back home I was offered a good job. I am now making good money and am able to provide for my wife and children. We have just bought new clothes and got ourselves all dressed up. I just want to say thank you for praying for my family and me. God is blessing us and we owe it all to you."

I said, "No, you owe it all to God. He is the great Healer and the great Savior. You came down from those mountains in faith and God has honored your faith. He is the One who deserves your praise."

It is wonderful to see God touch a person and heal them miraculously, but our Father doesn't stop there. He is in the business of transforming people's entire lives – for which we are incredibly grateful.

CHAPTER 25

God's Indescribable Grace

A shared mentor

In previous chapters I have already spoken about my friendship with pastor Eulogio Rivero, with whom we planted churches in Colombia. I want to share a little more of Eulogio's own amazing story to show how God's awesome grace is at work in the lives of every one of us.

Doris and I were based in the city of Barranquilla, Colombia, when I received a phone call from our friend, missionary Floyd Woodworth. He told me that a family who had been exiled from Cuba had arrived in the neighboring city of Cartagena. Floyd knew them because at one time he had been a missionary to Cuba, and this family had been pastoring churches there.

The authorities had expelled them from Cuba, exiling them to Spain. Arriving there, however, the Spanish authorities refused them entry and put them back on a ship headed for Cartagena, Colombia. Floyd told us that prior to their deportation they'd had to endure several years in a concentration camp in their own country. This poor, displaced family had now landed in Cartagena with nothing more than the clothes on their backs.

I immediately went to visit Cartagena and endeavored to locate them. It took quite some time. I did a lot of searching and asked a lot of questions. Eventually I found someone who had seen them and they pointed me to a small apartment in an area called the Plaza de los Coches.

The Rivero's children were about the same age as our children and we all became great friends. In due course we began to work and minister together. It was such a blessing to get to know and love this family.

Eulogio was the pastor of a church when the regime in Cuba, at that time, became increasingly repressive and began to persecute him and his family. The authorities pulled Eulogio out of his job as pastor and he spent the next three years in a concentration camp at one end of the island, being forced to labor each day cutting sugarcane.

His wife was taken to another part of the island and forced to work as a teacher. For three years they never saw each other once. They were reunited only when the government decided to put them on a ship and throw them out of the country.

As tragic as this story sounds, God had plans for the Rivero family, involving planting new churches in Colombia. They became an incredible support for our ministry and it was a blessing to have such quality people as this in the nation, working alongside us in pioneering ministry. We purchase land in Cartagena and began to run the crusade described in an earlier chapter. We then started working together to build a church. We were having a wonderful time in the Lord, enjoying one another's company and Christian fellowship in the city.

Eulogio and I had worked side by side for over a year when one day we had an amazing conversation. It reminded me again how expansive God's grace is, and how He miraculously weaves together individual lives and circumstances in order to accomplish His plans.

There was always something about Eulogio that reminded me of someone else. I couldn't put my finger on it, however, and couldn't come up with who that person was. One day, we were sitting together in his home and began to talk about the past.

Eulogio told me about his former pastor and Bible schoolteacher in Cuba and mentioned what a wonderful man he was. He didn't mention his name at this point. This early mentor had spoken clearly into his life and made a deep impression. Eulogio clearly loved and admired him.

We continued reminiscing about people who had been mentors to us and I began telling him about a man in Fort Worth, Texas, who had been such a blessing to me. He had spoken into my life a great deal and had given me opportunities to minister, so that I could learn and grow in my faith. I shared that he was also the man who had conducted our wedding. It was because

I mentioned Texas that Eulogio then referred to the name of his mentor:

"The man I'm talking about lives in the US and he is from Texas too. His name is Ed Anderson."

I couldn't believe my ears. I practically jumped out of my seat.

"You have to be kidding me! Did you say Ed Anderson?!"

It transpired that the same Ed Anderson, who had been my pastor and conducted mine and Doris' wedding ceremony, had been a pastor and Bible school lecturer to Eulogio. It was unbelievable that God had somehow connected us – two men with very different journeys, but with the same mentor and spiritual heritage.

All of a sudden it all made sense to me. I recalled that in years gone by Ed had been one of the first missionaries ever to go and pioneer churches in Cuba. At various points he had returned to the States, during which time he pastored the church I attended.

I smiled as I realized how Eulogio had taken on some of Ed's mannerisms whilst preaching. Ed Anderson had the habit of always rolling his right shoulder over and over whilst preaching. He would sort of roll his shoulders and jump around enthusiastically as he got into his message. When I watched Eulogio preach, he did exactly the same thing as he emulated Ed. That's why I always got the feeling that Eulogio reminded me of someone else. I just never imagined it could possibly be my old friend and pastor!

Here I was working with a man who had been exiled and shoved from country to country. He had become closer to me than a brother as we found ourselves laboring for the Lord in a nation foreign to both of us. We had been trained and taught by the same man. It shows me how God truly works out the situations and circumstances of our lives for the good of those who love Him and who are called according to His purposes (Romans 8:28). I realize that in the family of God we are all brothers and sisters and one day we are all going to come together.

A persecutor saved

Eulogio and I began to travel around the surrounding towns and villages of this part of Colombia. We did so in a way that perhaps sounds extraordinary now, compared to the way in which most Christian ministries function today. We would go into a village during the day, minister to the people to whom God directed us, and at night we would just sleep in the open countryside before moving on to the next place.

We ministered up and down the highways and byways of the area and, as evening closed, we would find a good site for a camp on a hillside. We would then build a bonfire to keep warm and string up our hammocks around it. We would talk and share stories about our lives late in to the night as we lay in our hammocks.

Eulogio told me more about his time of persecution in Cuba. Cuba had close links with Russia, who for years had endeavored to help Fidel Castro establish a communist regime, economically and politically.

So Eulogio found himself under Russian guard as he labored in the sugar plantation.

Each day he and his fellow prisoners were put to work in the sugar cane fields. The guards would treat them badly, beating them regularly for no reason other than to keep the prisoners in fear and themselves in control. Eulogio showed me the many scars he had acquired from his tormentors, up and down his arms and his back.

There was one guard, Eulogio said, who was more brutal and more feared than all the rest put together. He was always listening and watching. When he discovered that Eulogio was a Christian, he singled him out to be punished for his beliefs.

Eulogio was a faithful man of God and though unjustly incarcerated, he never quit telling others about Jesus. As he worked in the sugar cane fields, he sang and worshipped the Lord. Later, as he and the other men came together in the barrack-like buildings used for their living accommodation, different men would come to Eulogio and ask to hear about God.

"They would ask me to tell them about Jesus," he told me. "I would witness to them and offer to pray with some of them."

But he was never out of the scrutiny of this one guard who, as soon as he heard Eulogio speaking about Jesus, would intervene, break up the conversation, and brutalize him.

"If this man heard me sharing my faith or praying, he would come and grab me and beat me fiercely, telling me to shut up and stop talking about this Jesus. This happened regularly, but he would also catch me alone in the fields where again, he would just grab me and beat me into the ground."

Eulogio responded to this with Christ-like grace, love and forgiveness. He told me that every time he was beaten he would pray for that man – praying that God would have mercy on him and somehow reach him with His love. I thought that was awesome – that he could pray for the Lord to have mercy on the man who had treated him so appallingly. How like Jesus!

One day, after Eulogio and I had been working together for about two years, he came to me grinning from ear to ear. In fact, he was so excited to tell me some news that he could hardly stand still and was practically jumping up and down! I asked him what had gotten him so animated. He was holding a letter.

Incredibly, the letter had arrived with him via some friends in the US. It was written personally to Eulogio from the Russian guard who had singled him out for mistreatment and physical abuse, because of his faith.

The Russian wrote that he had been visiting the US and was spending time in New York. He was out one night, just walking around, getting to know the city when he heard music drifting out the window of a nearby building. "I realized that this music sounded like the songs you used to sing whilst working in the fields," he wrote.

"It used to make me so angry," the man wrote, "and I just had to shut you up. Then, when I heard you speaking about Jesus to the other men, your words pierced me and I would really hurt in my heart. I didn't understand why. I just knew I wanted to make you keep quiet, because I couldn't stand to listen to what you were saying."

Here in New York, as the man heard the sound of worship choruses being sung, he decided to go and investigate what it was all about. He slipped inside the door of a small church and sat at the back to observe. Inside he heard a man preaching, "...saying the same things I heard you saying in the barracks in Cuba." He told himself he was just going to find out what this was all about – purely out of interest – nothing more.

"But then I heard the preacher asking if anyone would like to come forward and receive Jesus Christ as their personal Savior. The man said, 'He will change your life.' I had no intention of becoming a Christian, but at that moment God touched me. I didn't understand what it was at first, though I understood later that it was the Holy Spirit. I found myself responding and going forward. That night I gave my heart to Jesus Christ."

The letter continued with these incredible words:

"I am now saved and filled with the Holy Spirit. The first thing that God told me to do was to find you. I have been looking for you for a long time to ask you to forgive me for the way I treated you, and for the terrible things I did to you and the other prisoners under my charge. As a Christian, I now understand why you would never be quiet and would continue to talk about the Lord Jesus. Please forgive me. I am now your brother in Christ and am asking you to forgive me for all the wrong thing I did to you."

As Eulogio and I read the letter again together, we just rejoiced and praised God. We thanked Jesus for this man's salvation and deliverance. Eulogio had been faithful in his service to Jesus and now another soul had been saved. In the same way that the apostle Paul was transformed from a persecutor of the brethren to a servant of Christ and a seeker of lost souls, we prayed that this man would be greatly used by God.

Once again we were astounded by and grateful for the awesome power of God and the way in which He extends His grace to people, no matter how far they have fallen.

CHAPTER 26

Peace in the Midst of the Storm

During life's journey each one of us will encounter and endure some storms; situations and circumstances that test our faith, sometimes threatening to overwhelm us. It is at such times that we must depend on the God who loves us, and trust Him to work everything out.

Through such trials and tribulations we discover the depth of God's love for us and, if we trust in Him, we will see that time and again He manages to birth miracles out of impossible situations. We will not always understand why we go through some of these things, but we know that our Father will always remain constant, loving and faithful.

He is always with us! As Psalm 23:4 puts so beautifully, *"Even though I walk through the valley of the shadow of death, I will fear no evil, for you are with me."* This is so comforting. David, the author of this psalm, reminds us that God is with us every step of the way, even in the most apparently dire of situations. The entire psalm speaks of God's peace. Even though we may find ourselves in a place of turmoil and confusion, God still operates in peace – because He is the embodiment of peace in Himself. And peace is what we so desperately need in the midst of any storm.

A storm hits

I experienced such a storm one time in Colombia. Our missions board had an evangelism and church planting strategy for Colombia that divided the country into three separate districts, with a superintendent put in place to oversee each one. I was elected to be the first superintendent of the North District.

As part of this role, I needed to go to the city of Santa Marta to set up a conference. We had already been very busy in the country planting churches, teaching in Bible schools, organizing church events, and conducting evangelism in many locations in the surrounding towns and villages. The purpose of the conference, which would span three days, was to bring together all of the pastors and workers involved for worship, fellowship and mutual encouragement. It was the first event of its kind in the region and we were all very excited about it. It was an opportunity to rally everyone together, allow God to speak into the lives of many people, and to share knowledge about the challenges of planting churches, answering people's questions.

Setting up and coordinating the conference some way from home meant that I had traveled to Santa Marta alone. It took a lot of time and effort and I had been away from my family for almost two weeks. But it was such a pivotal, important meeting that we wanted to be a great success, it was a sacrifice we all agreed was necessary.

Finally, the day came when the conference would commence and people would begin to arrive from all around the region. Pastors and workers were traveling from cities up and down the Caribbean Sea on the Colombian coast.

There was a knock on the door of the apartment where I was staying and I thought to myself, "Great! Some of the pastors are arriving early!" But when I opened the door I got a shock. There stood one of our young men. He had blood all over his clothes and his hands. He was shaking and weeping.

I can't describe the feelings I had at that moment – it was just so unexpected to see him in such a terrible condition. Stunned, I asked him what had happened to him. He unfolded to me a terrible tale that left me reeling.

On the journey to Santa Marta there had been a horrendous accident involving a truckload of pastors who had arranged to travel together. There had been a collision with another vehicle on the highway and the pastors' truck had spun out of control, turning over and over several times and literally scattering bodies up and down the road.

"Most of the pastors are dead," he told me gravely.

My mind raced. Doris and our daughters, Wynelle and Sharon, had also planned to travel with this same group out of the city of Barranquilla.

"What about my wife and two children?" I asked.

The young man said that they had also been killed in the accident. Suddenly, I felt numb and all alone. I hadn't seen or spoken to Doris and the girls in two weeks. Back then, communication was notoriously difficult. There were no cell phones, of course, but even landline phone communications were not good and it was virtually impossible to make city-to-city calls. Now I was being told by this young man that my wonderful wife and precious girls were likely dead.

The first thing I wanted to do was to get out of there and travel to the location of the accident as quickly as possible. Just then, the pastor of the local church we had established in Santa Marta arrived. The three of us got into my truck and set off for Cienega, the city where the crash had happened. It was an hour's drive away.

Throughout the journey I struggled to make sense of all this and cried out to God. I just kept thinking to myself, "How can this be? My wife, my children, the pastors – all dead?"

But the Lord is amazing. In this moment I knew a greater sense of God's presence as I found myself in the valley of the shadow of death, and I lived in the reality of the words of Psalm 23. Whilst in my mind I began to prepare myself for the worst, somehow God's peace filled my heart. The Bible says that the peace of God surpasses all understanding (Philippians 4:7). Looking back, though I can scarcely imagine myself in a worst storm, I can see how the supernatural power of God's peace overruled in that situation.

In due course we arrived at the scene of the accident and found everything still in great disarray. Nowadays, with sophisticated communications and well-equipped emergency services, such tragedies are dealt with swiftly. Not so in the Latin America of years gone by. It took a long, long time for information to filter through to the right people and for help to be provided.

As we arrived, after about one hour, one of my companions said to me, "Pastor Franklin, I don't think that your wife and children were in that truck." This comment was more than kind words, trying to reassure me. I believed it to be a spiritual insight. I took it as a great confirmation from the Lord.

There had been twenty people traveling together. Sadly, some of the pastors had died immediately in the crash. Others had suffered terrible injuries. They had broken bones or multiple fractures. Some had bones protruding from their shoulders, arms or ribs and were just lying by the roadside. I went from one person to the next, trying to discover the extent of their injuries.

As I was doing this, another vehicle linked to our group pulled up. The door opened and there was Doris, with our girls. In the end they had decided not to travel with the main group in the truck, since another missionary family had invited to ride with them. Words cannot describe the relief and thankfulness I felt that they were all okay.

As thankful as I was for the safety of my family, I also grieved for the loss of dear pastors and friends. Some of those who died were still students in Bible school who were training for ministry.

I located the only hospital in that town and went to speak with a doctor there. He gave me a long list of medicines that I would need to go and purchase at the local pharmacy. Again, in previous years in Latin America it was common practice that if you needed treatment, you would have to go personally to the pharmacy and buy the medication you needed, then take it to the hospital so that they could treat you. The hospitals simply did not stock the necessary medicines, and neither did they have the funding to go and purchase them. Many hospitals didn't even have the proper medical equipment necessary to do their job. It was just a part of life back then.

We decided that the best way to help the injured was to use my truck to transport those who could travel to the major city of Barranquilla. There, I knew, was one of the few hospitals that was better equipped with doctors and medical supplies. I could carry twelve people at a time in my truck.

We headed to Barranquilla. Don't picture us traveling down a modern highway though, because we had to travel on uncared for roads and often cross rivers where there was no bridge. At one point we arrived at the Magdalena River and had to sit there for a couple of hours, waiting for a ferry to come down the river. We had to drive up onto the ferry, go down the river at a very slow pace and then cross into Barranquilla on the other side.

There were a large number of vehicles on that ferry. As we sat there, trying to make our way to the hospital, people got out of their cars to come and look in the back of my truck. They could see this group of people with severe injuries and began asking questions, wanting to know what had happened. People were also astounded by the fact that this group of badly injured people were singing songs and glorifying God, even in the state they were in. "How can they be so happy when they are in so much pain?" people asked me.

Amazingly, in the midst of these strange circumstances, I was still able to minister to a few people who wanted to get to know this Jesus that the people were praising. Peace, in the midst of the storm! The testimony of these faithful pastors reached the hearts of people in need of God – and God graciously touched them.

There was a young lady called Carmen amongst our group. She was one of the most seriously injured of the survivors. Doris was looking after her as she lay on the front bench seat of the truck. She was a beautiful young lady of twenty-one, who was one of the students at the Bible school, and Doris had spent a lot of time mentoring her. It was such a tragic situation – we understood that Carmen had been caught underneath the truck as it literally rolled over her. She was now blind and crippled, since her head had been banged so hard that her optical nerves had been damaged, and her pelvic bone had been crushed, according to the doctor in Cienega. Doris and I just felt devastated for this lovely young woman with so much potential.

We eventually arrived at the hospital in Barranquilla and immediately medical staff began to take each one of the people in and take care of them, administering appropriate care and medication. We remained there for the rest of that day and on into the night.

Carmen was taken to a private area, screened by a curtain, so that the doctors could carry out a thorough evaluation of her injuries, examining her and taking x-rays. Doris and I decided to stay with her and waited outside to hear the opinion of the medical staff.

The night passed and the next day dawned before a doctor came to speak to us and invited us in to see Carmen. He confirmed what the other doctor had predicted, that her pelvic bone was crushed to the point where she had no feeling in her legs. We watched as he pricked her legs with a needle. Carmen confirmed that she couldn't feel anything. The doctor also confirmed that a severe blow to the back of her head had caused her to lose her sight.

"There is nothing anyone can do, other than wait and see how she recovers," he informed us.

We immediately asked the doctor if Doris and I could be alone with Carmen for a while to pray with her. "Yes, if you want," the doctor said, "but there is nothing you can do." I understood what he meant – but he didn't understand that we serve a mighty God who still hears and answers prayers. Some people may be beyond the help of medical intervention, but we serve a higher power!

Whilst Doris and I were praying for Carmen, she was speaking quietly under her breath. We thought at first she was praying along with us, calling out to God. Indeed, she was calling out to the Lord, but not for herself! We realized that she was speaking the names of the other people who had been injured: "God, please touch and heal Carlos..."

At one point I just had to stop her and ask her if she understood the severity of her own condition. "Carmen, you're praying for other people. You know that you are seriously ill?"

"Oh yes," she responded, "but I have to pray for the others – they are in a worse condition than I am."

Amazed at her selflessness, we continued to pray. Then, all of a sudden, we felt that supernatural peace of God flood in – the peace that only comes from Him because He *is* Peace.

Carmen was resting and Doris and I exited her room and stepped into the corridor. We stood talking for a while about what we would do next when the doctor came back. He came over to speak to us and it was at that moment that I heard Carmen calling my name.

"Brother Franklin ... Brother Franklin, look!"

When I turned around, there stood Carmen and we were all amazed to see her off the hospital bed, standing upright in front of us.

"Look!" she said, "I can walk! I can see!"

The doctor couldn't believe what he was witnessing. Carmen told us that as soon as Doris and I had left her, the awesome presence of God came into her room. "It was absolutely wonderful," she said. At that moment, her vision had returned and then she realized that feeling was flooding back into her legs. God had miraculously and instantaneously healed her. She was completely restored.

For some time the doctor was both speechless and motionless. He could not understand how someone with such terrible injuries could have been instantly healed and made well.

Now that she was healed, Carmen asked us to take her home. All three of us walked out of there and we put Carmen back in my truck to head to Soledad, the little town where she lived. All the way there she was laughing and praising God, saying, "I'm healed! I'm healed!"

Finally we arrived in Soledad. It was rainy and dark and Carmen's village was at the end of a dirt track. I couldn't see where I was going and the truck began to flounder in the rain-soaked mud.

"I don't think we are going to make it all the way to your house Carmen," I said.

"That's okay," she said, "I live right over there – just fifty yards away."

She thanked us for driving her home and then got out of the truck and walked down the muddy dirt track to her house, my headlights illuminating her way. Doris and I sat and watched her all the way into her house, holding hands. Doris turned to me and said,

"There goes a miracle."

And that is what she was – a walking miracle.

In months to come, Doris and I were privileged to perform Carmen's wedding to Roberto, one of our fine young pastors. Roberto and Carmen now pastor a church among the Guajira Indians in a very troubled area of Colombia, near the Venezuelan border. We just recently visited them there.

The accident occurred several years ago. Despite her amazing healing, the doctors told Carmen she would probably never be able to bear children, but God had other plans and they have four children! Now, some years later they have several grandchildren too. God is still using them and blessing them.

We serve a great God who gives us peace in the storms of life. No storm is too big or too fierce to be quelled by the peace of God. As the Lord Jesus calmed the waters for His disciples, so He calms the storms in our lives.

He hears our cry; He answers our call; He gives us peace.

We serve an awesome, powerful God who is the same yesterday, today and forever. Because He lives, we have the victory!

Epilogue

Rather than tell a chronological life story, through this book we have chosen to recount stories that highlight the goodness, faithfulness, and awesome power of the God we serve. We hope that the stories have sparked fresh faith in you and inspired you to believe for bigger and better things in your walk with God and your life of service to Him.

God has done some wonderful and amazing things during the course of our lives – and He is not done yet! Nothing would please or excite us more, however, than if our story inspired you to reach further and go higher than we did. We pray that God will bless you in all your endeavors for Him, and that you will know His peace, provision, protection and power in every part of your life.

As for us, we continue to go wherever the Lord leads.

God bless you.

Franklin & Doris Burns

Contact Information

You can find out more about Franklin and Doris' ministry by visiting their Facebook page at:

https://www.facebook.com/BurnsMinistriesInternational

Email: burnsministry@cs.com

Or,

bmispanish@embarqmail.com